PRAIS
MOTHERHOO

Juxtaposing tender mother-child moments with the dangers facing African American boys, Austin captures both the love and fear of her parenting experience in this powerful, spirited narrative.

—Publishers Weekly

Eye-opening, trenchant book, which helps to bolster the scant literature for African American adoptive parents that Austin has pioneered by blogging for publications such as *MUTHA* magazine and the *Huffington Post*...Austin's experiences, both positive and negative, are recounted in this fast-paced, heartwarming memoir of motherhood and adoption told through an African American lens.

—Library Journal, STARRED review

Austin challenges readers to question the ideal of motherhood as being synonymous with whiteness. Along the way, she tackles the inherent sexism, classism, and racism within the adoption system and the broader community...an essential addition to the literature about adoption, reflecting a viewpoint that is sorely lacking.

—Kirkus Reviews, STARRED review

A moving and necessary corrective to the primarily white narrative on adoption.

—Booklist

Both informational and inspiring, and is a much-needed addition to the literature of motherhood.

—*BookRiot*

Motherhood So White is a testament to the power of love as a radical act and an urgent call to reclaim motherhood from institutionalized whiteness.

—*BookPage*

A powerful memoir.

—Deesha Philyaw, *Literary Mama*

"*Motherhood So White* blew me away. Nefertiti's honest account of her unique journey to parenthood serves as a sharp reminder that in our society, parenting is not a colorblind experience. This is an important book for anyone committed to creating a more equal playing field for all our children."

—KJ Dell'Antonia, author of *How to Be a Happier Parent*

"Austin's frank voice and determined spirit speak truth to the media powers that present #MotherhoodSoWhite while relaying her history and thoughtful parenting decisions… A needed and important contribution."

—Meg Lemke, editor-in-chief of *MUTHA* magazine

"For the Black woman lost in the pale seas of mainstream mothering and adoption stories, *Motherhood So White* is a boat, life jacket, and first mate. [Austin] places her unique story in the larger context of parenting while Black, using her family's history and American history to ground a universal story of a woman finding her place as a mother. And knowing that motherhood can indeed be 'so white,' she opens her story to include the stories of other Black adoptive moms."

—Anthonia Akitunde, founder of Mater Mea

motherhood so white

A MEMOIR OF RACE, GENDER, AND PARENTING IN AMERICA

NEFERTITI AUSTIN

This publication is designed to provide accurate and authoritative information in regard
to the subject matter covered. It is sold with the understanding that the publisher is not
engaged in rendering legal, accounting, or other professional service. If legal advice
or other expert assistance is required, the services of a competent professional person
should be sought. —*From a Declaration of Principles Jointly Adopted by a Committee
of the American Bar Association and a Committee of Publishers and Associations*

This book is a memoir. It reflects the author's present recollections of experiences
over a period of time. Some names and characteristics have been changed, some
events have been compressed, and some dialogue has been re-created.

All brand names and product names used in this book are trademarks,
registered trademarks, or trade names of their respective holders. Sourcebooks
is not associated with any product or vendor in this book.

Published by Sourcebooks
P.O. Box 4410, Naperville, Illinois 60567-4410
(630) 961-3900
sourcebooks.com

Library of Congress Cataloging-in-Publication data is on file with the publisher.

Printed and bound in the United States of America.
VP 10 9 8 7 6 5 4 3 2 1

This book is dedicated to my grandparents:
Ann, Henry, Grandma, and Pop, for
setting the bar really high.

Contents

Prologue

"Come on, August, grab your pullover." I waited for my little boy at our front door.

"Where are we going, Mama?" August asked, dragging his black Gap sweatshirt behind him across the hardwood floors.

"To a rally at the park," I answered, sliding the hoodie over his tall, slender body. Handsome and inquisitive at only five years old, August already had the makings of a scientist/cowboy/race car driver, and I was proud of how far he had come.

In a past life, before we became a family, August had lived in two foster homes. Meanwhile, I earned a license to foster/ adopt from the Los Angeles Department of Children and Family Services. After months of certification and waiting, I became a mother to a six-month-old Black baby boy, and my life changed forever.

August's addition to the neighborhood made us one of five Black families who dwelled between La Cienega and San Vicente

Boulevard. August and I loved our little slice of heaven—filled with Mexican Jews, nonpracticing Jews, old people, Koreans, young white families, and a formerly handsome playboy, who drove a red convertible and didn't date anyone older than twenty-five—just outside of the Beverly Hills hub. La Cienega Park, with its green play structures, sandbox, clean bathrooms, and recreation center, was a block away. Every day, elderly Jewish men sat at concrete benches, speaking Hebrew, feeding pigeons, and playing chess. Mothers nursed their babies or worked out with trainers, and little kids played king of the hill. On Wednesdays, the park was filled with divorced and coparenting dads and their children. The rumor was that Wednesday was designated court-ordered visitation day. Every now and then, a B-list celebrity from *The Fast and the Furious* would be on dad duty.

Before I adopted August, I landed in Beverly Hills in June 2006 on a fluke. I had lived in the San Fernando Valley for seven years when the condominium I was previously renting was sold. I was in denial about moving and waited until the last possible moment to find a place, when I stumbled upon a one-bedroom apartment on the eastern border of Beverly Hills. There were no fancy shops near me, and if I wanted to stargaze or stroll down Rodeo Drive, I'd have to drive west on Wilshire Boulevard for eight minutes. It wasn't the most upscale apartment building either, and even my grandmother made sure to emphasize to her sister and church members that we didn't *really* live in Beverly Hills, but it was home.

As we made our way down the dusty steps and onto the street, August asked, "What's a rally?"

"It where lots of people who like the same things come together and talk or sing." Earlier that morning, I had googled the Black Lives Matter website to see when they were coming to Los Angeles. As I scrolled down the page, I discovered a rally that night. I was frankly surprised a rally would be held in Beverly Hills. Of course, there was wealth in the area, but this was not a fund-raiser. It was an event that was designed to bring white people, far removed from blight, gangs, and poverty, out into the street in support of Black lives. It was one thing to send money or sit at home and hand-wring. It was another to publicly cry foul at a system that routinely oppressed Black people. That's what I had done by adopting August, and that was the reason I took him out that night.

"Like a party?" His eyes lit up.

My child was not even in kindergarten and already a party animal. "Um, not really." It was already seven o'clock. Ordinarily, August would be getting into a warm, sudsy bath at this time of the evening. After he played with his boats and fish, he'd be ready for a cup of milk. Then August, who liked brushing his teeth, would delay bedtime by splashing water all over the sink. While I cleaned up, he would choose three or four books from his overflowing red-and-blue bookcase and wait for me in his twin bed. Tonight, I was disrupting his routine for one reason. I needed to connect with other mothers of Black boys.

"Why are we going?"

Good question. My heart echoed President Obama's sentiment that Trayvon's murder was a *national tragedy*. This was one of the few moments in history that the death of a Black boy was elevated to a national tragedy. I took a beat to consider how to broach the subject. If I gave my sensitive child too much information, he would feel bad without understanding why. If I gave too few details, he would miss the importance of the moment. I did not want to frighten him, but lying wasn't the answer either.

"Why, Mama?" he asked again.

"Because a few weeks ago, a boy named Trayvon Martin was killed walking home, and we want to show our support."

I spoke calmly, hoping to give August the impression that despite using the words *boy* and *killed*, my son was safe. I pretended we were just taking a casual stroll to the park, though the circumstances were far from normal. Except, I quickly realized, they were normal. *This* was my new normal. Most Blacks were taught that life was tenuous and this reality was just part of living in America. Before becoming a mother, I was detached from what that really meant. I lived in an affluent neighborhood and ran with a highly educated, well-traveled crowd. I thought my privilege shielded me from ugly truths about the actual worth of a Black life. Trayvon Martin's murder opened my eyes to the new reality Black mothers faced every day. There was no guarantee that our boys would arrive home safely from school or back from the store after purchasing Skittles.

Trayvon's death grounded my parenting priorities. I went

from trying to understand the difference between the Montessori and the Reggio Emilia approaches to education, to understanding that I was part of a club whose sole membership requirement was being the mother of a Black boy, and feeling the weight of that fear keenly for the first time. Suddenly, I was scared for August, who shared a birthday with Dr. Martin Luther King Jr. I wept inside because there would be times in August's life when trouble would find him, even if he was just out minding his own business, all because his racial classification was Black. Trayvon's death gave me another thing to worry about: life. How could I protect my son? How could I give him the best life, one where he enjoyed a childhood of trains and dinosaurs, not rallies for the gone-too-soon? In my new skin as mother of a Black boy, I had to think through how we would navigate a world set up to challenge his very existence. The task was daunting and made me feel powerless and small.

"Mama, I don't know Trayvon. He must be in Miss Isabella's class."

"No, he was a big boy," I said softly.

"What does *kill* mean?"

I had seen that one coming. "*Kill* means..." I faltered and tried again. "Um, killing is like when you step on ants and they die."

August frowned. "Did someone step on Trayvon? That's mean."

"I don't know all of the details, but—" I lied to stop the hole of fear that was swallowing me. "There are some mean people in the world, and a mean man killed Trayvon."

"Will that happen to me?"

I stopped walking and bent down, cupping August's face in my hand, and looked into his beautiful brown eyes. "Oh no, angel, but you need to know that some people will think just because you're a Black boy that you are not smart and funny. They will not care how much you love Elmo or how you got angry when you found out Pluto was a dwarf planet."

"Why?" he asked sadly.

"I don't know. Some people are stupid."

"Ooh, you said a bad word."

"Oops!" I covered my mouth and pretended to giggle.

"Can I get on the slide when we get to the park?" August was hopeful.

"Not tonight, son."

I'm not sure if he understood that I had just done something terrible, had stolen some of his innocence. I had no choice. In ten years, August would be more than six feet tall, and people would assume he was older than he really was. He would not be given the "boys will be boys" benefit of the doubt for speeding or participating in immature class pranks. Trayvon's murder unleashed a veil that separated August's previous life as a precious, innocent babe to a child who would have to learn that his race and gender could get him killed.

Our busy street, a shortcut to the Beverly Center and West Hollywood, was quiet for once. The corner our apartment building sat on also held three office buildings, though the low brick building that used to house a colonic clinic was vacant. The rumor was that nearby Cedars-Sinai Hospital had purchased the prime location and would begin demolition of the old building soon.

I had made this trek to the park hundreds of times. First, as a single woman, newly arrived in Beverly Hills, walking my dogs, then, as a single mother pushing August in his stroller. Later, August would push his own stroller, and I would watch him stumble and fall, learning to walk and trying to keep up with our dogs. The park was our haven where he spent time building sandcastles, making friends, and learning to ride his bike. But tonight, we had other business there.

With no cars in sight, August scampered ahead and waited for me at the streetlight. The light was red, so he pressed the button to illuminate the walk signal. The intersection of Wilshire Boulevard and Gale Drive felt like a cold wind tunnel. Concerned about the cool night air, I gently turned him to face me.

"Angel, let's pull your hood over your head."

Suddenly, the reality of our situation hit me. We were Black people, dressed in dark colors, standing on a street corner in a wealthy neighborhood. I had a brief moment of panic and contemplated removing August's hood and warming him through my embrace. I knew that a white boy wearing a hoodie wouldn't warrant a second look from a passerby. August was young enough that he could get away with it, but if he were, say, thirteen, he would likely be perceived as threatening with his hood up. To the white world we lived in, a hoodie plus a Black male was synonymous with danger.

I grimaced at the irony that I could not even get to the park to protest the death of a Black teenager without considering how August would be perceived. I decided to let it be and keep his hood up. We had not done anything wrong.

Trayvon's murder spoke to all aspects of my identity: Black woman, single Black mother, historian, sister, cousin, coworker, friend, lover. Much as I would have liked to, I could not ignore what was happening to Black boys all around me, or rationalize the violence away to convince myself that August would be spared. As an adjunct United States and African American history instructor at multiple Los Angeles community colleges, I was well versed in how this shit played out. So many Black men had been lynched and killed at the hands of white men in America. It was a record on repeat, a song I tired of, especially now that I had a son to raise.

My pedigree and privilege gave me access to a world away from police brutality, drugs, incarceration, and premature death. I had collected stamps on my passport from three continents, been to law school, explored slave castles in West Africa, walked in the footsteps of the Harlem Renaissance's elite on Martha's Vineyard, rafted down the Guadalupe River, and been to the flash point of the Civil War in South Carolina. I had danced atop tables at beach retreats in Mexico, sunned on whimsical weekend trips in Palm Springs, changed cars and jobs every other year, and maintained standing hair and massage appointments. I was a free, successful Black woman in the world, and still, none of that meant my child would surely be spared the fate of so many Black boys in our country. I wanted August to have the same privileges I did, but a case of mistaken identity or racial profiling could wreck all of that. That's not what I had signed up for when I decided I wanted to become a mother.

I was already an outlier in the Black community for adopting a child I did not know and was not related to. I was an outlier in the white community for adopting a child domestically and the butt of jokes by male coworkers who didn't believe I could raise a boy on my own. As a writer, I was fighting against white privilege's erasure of Black parenting perspectives and insistence that the word *mother* automatically meant *white*. The denial of voices of color meant our children's lives did not matter. Motherhood was supposed to be fun, filled with challenges to bring the best out of our kids and ourselves. For me, and for all Black mothers in America, it was alternatively fun and harrowing, as we broached conversations no parent should ever have to have with their young children.

As the death of Black boys became a way of life, my eyes opened to an important truth: Black mothers lived in a different America from white mothers. I saw the ease with which my white mom friend Liza babied her five-year-old son, Colton. While she closely monitored his emerging reading skills, she failed to educate him about the fact that America had a Black president. She had no idea that toy guns in the hands of Black boys could be misconstrued as a threat. Colton was free to roam about the country at will; August had to be vigilant about where he was at all times.

When we finally arrived at the park, most of the protestors were gone. We missed it. I hadn't known what to expect but was willing to walk into a scene of grief, anger, shouting, and volatility. That was not the case. It was as if providence wanted me to keep August's innocence intact a little longer. I was disappointed but relieved and happy to have shown up, not just for August but for all mothers of Black boys.

August asked, "Where are the people?"

I looked at the throng of footprints in the sand and noticed a few stragglers sitting quietly at the tables where the old Jews played chess. "They've gone home," I said, kissing his cold cheek. "Thanks for being such a trooper tonight."

"Now, can I get on the slide? Please."

"No, sir." I winked. "You need to get some rest so you'll be ready for school tomorrow."

I took my job as mother seriously, not only teaching August how to tie his shoes or his ABCs, but teaching him about the institutional racism that was and would be a part of his life. No matter how fancy our zip code, he would need that information to stay alive. Now woke to the broader meaning of Black motherhood, I turned inward…to adoption. This path was not easy for a Black woman wanting to parent in America, where motherhood was filtered through a white lens.

My Adoption So Black

My parents, Diane and Harold, met in Los Angeles in 1968 at the Watts Field Center, an employment agency where they were both looking for jobs. Diane was nineteen years old and dating another guy who belonged to the cultural nationalist United Slaves or Us Organization, founded by Dr. Ron Karenga, creator of Kwanzaa. The organization was pro-Africa with a strong emphasis on the Black family. Though my dad hated Karenga, he respected his ideas about Black economics. The ideals of Black nationalism appealed to both Diane and Harold, whose respective square parents were desperately trying to keep them on the straight and narrow.

Diane's parents, Ann and Henry Hawthorne, migrants from the segregated South, wanted Diane to go to college and get a job. Harold's parents, John Sr. and Doris Austin, also southerners, wanted the same for their son. Diane wanted to be free to live her life as she saw fit. In Harold, she found a kindred spirit, and she eventually left her boyfriend to marry him. They wanted to create a life and home where art, music, and political thought triumphed over racism and capitalism, where Black would be beautiful every day and where they were recognized as equal citizens in America.

The Hawthornes, my grandparents, were humble about the success they had managed to attain despite their challenging circumstances. With dreams of a better life, Henry had relocated from Beaumont, Texas, and Ann from Boyle, Mississippi, in the 1940s. They both had a strong Protestant work ethic and did not curse or drink. They saved their money, took care of their children, and enjoyed the trappings of a middle-class existence in California. My mother and her sister, Helen, took ballet and tap dance lessons, and their brother, Eldridge, was a Boy Scout. They attended a predominantly Black United Methodist church in Baldwin Hills, with parishioners who spoke in hushed tones in the sanctuary. They took family vacations to Bryce Canyon, Yellowstone National Park, Beaumont, and Mississippi, often with their first cousin, Ray, in tow. Ann and Henry believed that if a person got a good education and worked hard, they, too, would have the American dream of home ownership, family, annual vacations, and a cushy retirement.

Middle child Diane was unimpressed by her family's history or conventional lifestyle. In her mind, her parents were out of touch with the times and woefully unprepared for how drastically the world was changing. Despite showing early signs of potential, she wanted no part of their bourgeoisie lifestyle. Diane had been valedictorian of her junior high school in Compton, but became defiant when the family moved to predominantly white Windsor Hills for her to attend high school. Her rebellion started with running away from home to see friends in Compton, smoking cigarettes, and stints in juvenile hall, and she finally moved out of Ann and Henry's home before graduating from Dorsey High School.

A love child, I entered the world four days before Neil Armstrong landed on the moon and Miles Davis's *Bitches Brew* became the first important jazz fusion album. Two years later, Coca-Cola launched a juggernaut ad replete with multicultural faces singing about buying the world a home and furnishing it with love. Their perfect harmony belied the Black and Brown Vietnam veterans returning home, strung out on heroin, dazed, confused, and unable to find employment. America in the 1970s had blood on its hands from riots that had engulfed Los Angeles, Newark, Detroit, and other metropolitan cities during the previous decade. White women were demanding equal rights. Black women were finding their voices; Huey Newton was free; Angela Davis was on trial for her life, and Assata Shakur had disappeared into the arms of Cuba. My brother, Kareem Ali, arrived exactly two and a half years later in January 1972. By that time, our parents were married and trying to raise a family.

My parents cut their teeth during this turbulent climate. Harold and Diane had separately melted into the Black Power movement by rejecting their parents' lifestyles. They wanted to uplift the Black race through protest, pride in their African heritage, jazz, poetry about revolution, and drugs that gave them freedom from what was going on. They saw themselves as the proletariat and, like many young people, were seduced by the powerful rhetoric of those unafraid of *the man*. My dad was so entrenched in wanting power for the people that his best friend christened him Seibu Jahid-Ali, a name my dad took to mean *warrior*, though the secondary translation would be *exalted, hardworking man*.

My father, Harold, was also a middle child. His family moved west from Watts to a three-bedroom home in southwest Los Angeles. This neighborhood was filled with three- and four-bedroom homes, large backyards, great schools, and whites who took flight in 1960. His parents and my mom's parents moved west to give their children a running start at the American dream. They had aspirations for their children and thought that a life grounded in Christianity, family, and love was all they needed to navigate the dystopian 1960s. What my grandparents didn't know was that their middle-class values were no match for the burning desire my father and many others had to hold white folks accountable, or the subsequent call of the streets. After he was put out of his parents' home, he went to live with his aunt Dee. While there, he attended community college, partied, and worked odd jobs until meeting my mother. He was happy when he learned she was pregnant and told me many times, "I just knew you were a boy." Surprise!

When Kareem and I were very young, our family lived in a small apartment in Inglewood. My mother worked nights, and sometimes while she was at work, my dad made me and my brother peanut butter-and-honey sandwiches and Kool-Aid. My dad was handsome, charismatic, athletic, and troubled, with a drug problem he was never able to shake, anger management issues, and dreams that never came to pass.

He tried to make sense of the unpredictable world he inhabited and found solace in books like Chancellor Williams's *The Destruction of Black Civilization* and Frantz Fanon's *The Wretched of the Earth*. He was an avid reader of all things related to Africa, slavery, Marxism, segregation in the United States, and had an amazing jazz record collection. My love of art and sense of equality came from his passions and romantic sensibilities. I grew up believing that he was a member of the Black Panther Party, but it wasn't until he died that I discovered he had actually joined the Black Vanguard, a group more radical than the Panthers.

At our Inglewood apartment, the record player was always spinning and my parents' friends would come over and smoke weed, snort cocaine, drink Gallo wine, and dance to Marvin Gaye into the wee hours. Kareem and I were supposed to be in bed, but we couldn't sleep with the loud music and laughter of high adults in the house. Sometimes, we would crawl to the doorway and watch. I was five years old and curious about what antics they were up to.

Harold and Diane's young, chaotic love and volatility forced me to mature early. Kareem and I were left alone a lot, and our parents slept heavily. In the mornings after their parties, five or six adults would be passed out in the living room, and we'd have to step over them to get to the kitchen to pour ourselves some cereal. It was up to me to take care of Kareem, so I would be in charge of making breakfast or a snack. Too short to reach the Cheerios on top of the fridge, I'd stand on a chair and hand Kareem the box. Then I'd get the heavy gallon jug from the fridge and pour milk into a bowl, trying not to spill. I was mothering when my mother could not.

Other times, our parents' arguments left us afraid. They cussed each other out, and I have at least one memory of Harold hitting Diane. By 1974, their marriage was over. My dad went to the penitentiary, my mom went to rehab, and we went to live with Ann and Henry.

When Kareem and I were a little older, my Afroed daddy would take us to MacArthur Park, where he'd blow poetry about love, loss, and the people. In addition to writing, he could build or fix anything, and was a talented photographer and forger of driver's licenses. It took a steady hand to laminate those little cards, and he honed his craft in the early 80s in prison, practicing gemology and earning a certificate from the Gemological Institute of America. Over the course of my childhood and adolescence, he worked as a youth counselor, car salesman, sold Amway, and performed a myriad of other jobs that did not require a college degree. The few jobs he had generally ended with him getting fired or quitting because he wasn't making enough money. So, he hustled.

Harold generally kept us away from his drug dealing, but there were times when we'd be visiting with him and he'd tell us that he had to make a *run*. That was code for us to wait in the car, or if it was night and we were spending the night with him, that he was going out and would not return until early the next morning. He knew we wouldn't leave the apartment or tell our grandparents what he was up to. That would have caused all kinds of hell to break loose. Nor did we share with our Windsor Hills classmates that our dad had guns hidden within the couch, smoked weed in front of us, or had us wait in the car while he made a run. I doubt he was proud of how he made money, but as a felon without a college degree and a drug addiction, his choices of employment were slim, and he did what he had to do.

What Harold should have been was a historian. The stories he told us about his younger years with our mother made their lives seem dangerous, exciting, like watching a Blaxploitation film for kids. Without realizing it, he gave me the ability to imagine a creative life, and his way with words later carried me through my career. I felt like he saw me, and that it was important that I knew who he was. In contrast, my mother was silent on the subject of her past. Perhaps this was why my parents were a good match. Unless Diane and her sister, Helen, were laughing about their glory days in 1968 as stone foxes in the Kwanzaa parade, my mother did not share anything about herself. So, I only got one side of their story and learned my history through Harold's eyes.

I had to depend on other people's memories to construct a full picture of Diane as a person, but one of the strongest memories I have is about my name. My parents never agreed over who named me, but it was important to my mother that I be able to spell the complicated syllables. Fully able to read and write since I was three years old, I still could not spell my name in kindergarten. One night, when we still lived in Inglewood, I was attempting to complete a worksheet for school.

Diane took a drag off her cigarette and patted her short, perfectly rounded Afro. Dressed in blue jeans, extra-large hoop earrings, and a white back-out that complemented her rich brown skin, Diane was every inch a 1970s soul sista.

"Write your name at the top," my mother prompted. She was frying potatoes in a cast iron skillet.

"I don't know how," I whined. I sniffed and wiped tears from my chubby cheeks. I hated all nine clumsy letters. *N-E-F-F-E-T-I-T-I*, my parents' spin on Nefertiti, queen of Egypt.

Diane took a steak knife to sharpen my pencil and wrote my name across the top. "Copy these letters. Do it ten times."

Kids and adults alike had a hard time pronouncing my name, and most had never heard of my royal Egyptian namesake. The African/Arabic names my parents had bestowed on me and Kareem invited jokes and merciless teasing. In the late 1960s and early 1970s, Afrocentric parents like mine often assigned their kids names like Africa, Jabari, Ali, and Kente. That was all well and good in the confines of the movement, but it became a huge problem in my bourgeoisie neighborhood filled with names like Charisse, Toiya, Laurie, Anthony, and David.

My mother, who was angry that I did not like my name, said, "We wanted you to be your own queen."

"But the other kids tease me, and my teachers don't say it right," I complained. I was so done with being called *Left Titty*, *Miss Kitty*, and *Ne-fetti* that I changed my name to Tina in the third grade.

My father, who was equally unsympathetic to my plight, said, "I got that name from Miles Davis's last acoustic album: *Nefertiti*."

I did not care. As a child, the origins of my name held no significance, and I vowed when I grew up and had kids, I would never give them stupid names.

My parents got a Black divorce, which meant they physically and emotionally went on with their respective lives, but neither legally filed for divorce. This arrangement was common in the Black community, because a formal divorce involved lawyers, which meant a lot of money had to be spent to make a separation legal. If kids had been produced during a marriage, divorce was a direct pipeline to family court and child support, which could result in a father going to jail for missed payments. Many Black women did not want to see their child's father imprisoned or buried in so much debt that he couldn't contribute financially or emotionally to his kids' lives, and an inherent distrust of the justice system throughout the community made it preferable to handle separations in a more informal way.

My parents' permanent separation marked the first time

my brother and I lived with our grandparents, Ann and Henry. Spending time with them was fun. We helped Ann pick strawberries from her garden, and Henry would challenge us with simple counting and spelling games. They even went along with my parents' progressive foolishness and taught us to call them by their first names, instead of Grandmother and Grandfather. They were happy my parents' relationship was over and hoped their daughter was on the road to ditching the drama of her younger years and becoming a responsible mother.

After Diane got out of rehab, we went back to live with her, but the arrangement didn't last long. For the next four years, we moved from Inglewood to Ann and Henry's home to Gardena and back again, switching school districts along the way. My mother was clean for short stints but never stable enough to provide a real home for us. She was leading a life of crime: boosting clothes from Broadway department stores, transporting drugs for her boyfriend, and God knows what else. Parenting was not a priority.

I distinctly remember being eight years old and watching Diane sing along to Billie Holiday's "Ain't Nobody's Business If I Do" and Johnny Guitar Watson's "Ain't That a Bitch," as she cleaned our apartment on Stepney Street in Inglewood during one of the periods in which we lived with her. She would be snapping her fingers and off in her own world. We had bright yellow patio furniture, a glass-and-brass coffee table, and a black poodle named Peppy. My mom worked on and off, and pretty much let us run wild. Most of her boyfriends were nice, but they were drug dealers or some other form of lowlife. Just like Harold had, she'd take us on a run, or we'd sit for hours at someone else's house, listening to music or playing outside while she got her swerve on. Diane was also drinking heavily, on welfare, and unable to keep a job. Naturally, we did not tell our grandparents. We protected her, even when she didn't protect us.

My father was in the same boat. Most of his crimes were drug-related, and he was in and out of jail. Harold was a convicted felon, which meant he struggled to get a legitimate job outside of construction or at low-paying nonprofit youth organizations aimed at deterring young people from life on the streets. Though he could build anything, he felt that manual labor was beneath him. My dad had delusions of grandeur, believing that one day he'd buy a home in Windsor Hills and we'd all live together again. It was an odd dream for a man who had ardently rejected his parents' bourgeoisie lifestyle. I can only guess that as a father, he finally realized his children needed stability, and at the rate he was going, he would never be able to offer it to us.

When we lived with Diane, we always looked forward to going to Ann and Henry's house, a mid-century home in upper middle-class Windsor Hills. Ann would prepare us a quick meal, usually chicken and greens, followed by dessert. There was always a carton of vanilla ice cream in the freezer, iced oatmeal cookies, or frosted animal crackers in the cookie jar. Ann was serious about her garden and taught us how to pick strawberries without bruis-ing them from the patch on the side of the house. Henry would either be reading the newspaper or a DIY book on nutrition, or typing a letter on his forty-pound black Royal typewriter that no one, including Ann, was allowed to touch.

If Ann and Henry weren't home when we stopped by, sometimes a brown sack awaited us on their doorstep. Henry would use a black marker to write our names and draw a happy face on each bag. Usually, a green apple and pastry were inside, showcasing a small token of grandparently love. Growing up, the gift offered joy and stability amid the chaos of life with our drug-addicted mother and father. At that point, Kareem and I were unaware that our situation would soon change dramatically. One day, when we were nine and six years old, we'd climb those steps and find not a sack lunch but home. Home, as in a permanent living situation. Home, as in we would no longer be raised by our parents. Home, as in my own Black adoption, a nonlegally binding agreement executed between Ann, Henry, Grandma, Pop, Harold, and Diane. Though we were never formally adopted, our entire family, and the rest of the world, would soon recognize Ann and Henry as our parents.

———————

If Ann and Henry had any complaints about becoming parents again, they never said so. I, however, was ashamed of my parents' instability and absence. I realized something was wrong with our lives when we lived with our parents. We were at the bottom of their list of priorities, and that hurt.

I quickly discerned that life with Ann and Henry was light years better than the environment of ripping and running I was used to. I felt it in the peaceful quiet of our Windsor Hills home, and our steady routine of school, activities, chores, homework, dinner, bedtime. In the pat on the back from Henry, who was a germophobe and uncomfortable hugging anyone, and in the home-cooked meals Ann prepared every night. Their devotion was palpable and warm, just like the constant heat in the house, a warm, dry musk radiating from the floor furnaces in the living room, hallway, and den, a combination of heat convection and my grandfather's homemade humidifier. My grandfather always kept a metal pot of water in the well of the furnace to diffuse the dry air. Sometimes, he would remove them to show my brother, Kareem, and I the white-and-green chalky buildup clinging to the bottom and sides of the pots. He'd chip little pieces off, letting us touch the rough mineral deposits. Henry explained how calcium and magnesium built up over time and reminded us not to open the nickel-louvered wall grates. These impromptu science lessons were typical of his parenting style. He was a purveyor of knowledge on everything from how the body digested food to why what we saw on television was a pack of lies.

The high heat, prompting everyone who climbed the thirteen steps to the front door to quickly shed jackets and sweaters, wasn't the only constant in our home. The crackling of pork bacon teaming in a cast iron skillet every morning was another certainty. My grandmother always cut the package of bacon in half and insisted that a long-handled fork was the only tool needed to turn the meat. Her mother-in-law thought it was *country*, but Ann said cutting the bacon was the only way the pieces would fit neatly in the skillet. Bacon disappeared fast, and even Henry, who was a pescatarian, would snatch a piece if there was any left.

Evenings were reserved for the vinegary smell of collard greens and sweet Jiffy cornbread. Greens were Ann's favorite meal and she did not play when she made them. CNN was usually on in the background, and the oven door was left slightly ajar to let the warmth escape into the kitchen. Earlier in the day, she would have picked the giant leaves from her garden, meticulously removing every twig and pebble, and then washed the greens in the kitchen sink. While they soaked, Ann would grab her cast iron skillet and put a little water in the bottom to simmer a smoked turkey wing until the meat fell off the bone. This could take an hour. While the meat cooked, Ann pulled the leaves from the stalk, tossed what she didn't need, and then gathered garlic salt, black pepper, sliced onion, and Lawry's seasoning salt. The aluminum stove top pressure cooker would appear from a deep cabinet, and she'd combine the turkey wing with its hot gravy, seasonings, and enough water to cover the collards. She would lock the handle of the pressure cooker and let the steam work its magic. The *whisk-whisk* from the steam valve could be heard throughout the house, like a comforting whisper.

On the surface, our activities mirrored white middle-class America: a secure household, church, piano lessons, and baseball.

That should have been enough to take the sting out of my alternate family configuration, but it didn't. Peer approval, real and perceived, was important to me, and I felt embarrassed that almost all of my friends, Black and white, lived with both parents, or at least their mothers. My family felt different, and not in a good way.

Fortunately, my friends did not made fun of my living situation, but they were definitely curious. "Why don't you live with your mother?" was a standard question that I might be asked on the school bus or during a game of hopscotch or tetherball. There was no escaping the inquiry. My mom had a new man, with whom she relocated to Houston, Texas, with in 1981. I don't remember her leaving. There was no party, no tears, nor a discussion about her moving two thousand miles away. She was just gone.

Before Diane moved to Texas, I'd deflect my friends' curiosity. "We see her all the time." The adults around us were too busy in the day-to-day of child-rearing to sit down and explain why my mother didn't seem to want to live with us. I was left to use my imagination to come up with an answer that did not beget more questions.

After my mom moved, I'd say, "She moved to Texas, and we wanted to stay here." That answer carried some truth and gave me control over our family narrative. It also shut down any follow-up questions, except, "Where is your dad?"

My response to that one depended on whether or not he was in jail at the time. I might say, "Oh, he got a job up near Magic

Mountain or in Stanislaus." That meant that his decision to move was not up to him. My dad made a point to see us but spent the next twelve years in and out of jail. Even when he wasn't incarcerated, he was dealing drugs or making fake driver's licenses and flaking on the weekends he was supposed to see us. He never kicked his drug habit and was hooked on heroin when he was murdered in 1991, a victim of his own misdeeds and Black men's expendability in America.

Even with my grandparents' love and support, I felt inadequate. I was petite, looked younger than my years, and had a funny name. Our living arrangement did not have a formal definition, and no one told me that my Black adoption followed an established cultural tradition with its roots tracing back hundreds of years to Africa. Multigenerational family units in Africa included extended family, and at the center were the elders who held considerable social authority. We brought these ideas of family structure to America, though they would be tested for the next four hundred years under the institution of American slavery, Jim Crow segregation, mass incarceration, HIV, and AIDS.

Africans brought to America were used for two purposes: free labor and reproduction. Personal relationships were not acknowledged, let alone valued, as separation of family members began before Portuguese, British, and American slave ships set sail from Gorée Island, Elmina, Osu Castle and at least forty-five other slave ports. Men and women were purchased and then stolen from the African continent and forced to build infrastructure for the rapidly expanding American nation, breaking apart the multi-generational family structure that most African people knew. This separation led to fractured and manufactured family units among the Black community in America. Untethered Black people without relatives to greet or house them made family on the farms and plantations where they were sold. Blood ties carried less significance because relationships between slaves were uncertain and often dependent upon the success or failure of cotton, sugar, or rice production in a particular region. Socially, the institution of slavery disavowed long-lasting connections between Blacks by making marriage between slaves illegal, as a reminder that they did not own themselves. And the perpetuation of fractured family units did not end with the Civil War.

Nineteenth- and twentieth-century sharecropping compounded fragile post-antebellum relationships between Black men and women, though marriage at least was legal. Sharecropping amounted to de facto slavery for unskilled laborers. Illiterate and powerless, farmers were duped into signing leases with egregious interest for animals, seeds, cabins, furniture, clothing, and fertilizer. With high debt, rigged balance sheets, and no other way to earn money, Black men and women were shackled to land they would never own. Many ran off in search of work and fair payment, leaving children and spouses destitute and defenseless. The need to survive overturned the ideals of African communal living. Sharecropping broke this traditional family value and made it impossible for the Black community to build neighborhoods, schools, or collectively shake off the dregs of slavery.

During the Great Migrations of the 1930s and 1940s, nearly six million Blacks left the South and headed north or west for jobs to get as far away from lynching, second-class citizenship, domestic terrorism, and social and economic discrimination as they possibly could. The wartime economy beckoned, and family members sent glowing letters home about their prosperity up North, causing many Blacks to abandon farm work for better financial opportunities and educational options. They found work in the defense industry, auto manufacturing, navy shipyards, and other skilled positions. In cities, Black women found jobs in restaurants and hospitals, and as teachers, and riveters on ships headed to combat, though many were forced to work as domestic help.

While these opportunities seemed to help heal the Black family unit, Black men had a hard time obtaining skilled or permanent positions or advancing in their professions due to the presence of white immigrants and the continued discrimination against people of color. Furthermore, limited education resources, especially for those coming from the segregated South, put the Black community at a disadvantage from the start, leading to discriminatory hiring practices and limited opportunity.

Upon discovering that the land of milk and honey was hostile, some men returned south for guaranteed, if physically laborious, work on farms. These Black men would stay connected to the family unit that remained north, sending back money when they could. This idea of the working parent, both in the North and the South, created a new kind of family dynamic. Geographically,

Dad was elsewhere, and Mom, now a single parent and most likely working as a maid, was not available to support her own children. Who was left to raise the children? Relatives or neighbors in similar situations. These migrants were connected by circumstance, and the community that surrounded the unit became an extension of *family*.

The practice of raising nieces, nephews, cousins, and grandchildren was soon ingrained in Black households and the main reason Black people formally adopted at lower rates than whites did. Calling back to the multigenerational family unit of precolonial Africa, we did not need social workers or dependency court, just the blessing of the elders to raise a child within our community.

Black adoption had one other rule: a point of reference. The family taking in the child needed a connection with that child, even a tenuous one. We needed to be able to point to behavior, coloring, or height, and directly attribute those factors to a known or somewhat known parent, as opposed to taking in a stranger's child. White people took in strangers—we did not. Even though I didn't know it as a young girl, my family was fulfilling a cultural model created for us by our ancestors.

———

Life with Ann and Henry was good. Bussing had come to the Los Angeles Unified School District just in time for me to take advantage of it. The Triad Program, a volunteer initiative to increase diversity in public schools had started, and I, along with other Black kids from Windsor Hills, were bussed to mostly white Westchester for fourth and sixth grades. The white kids from Westchester were bussed to predominantly Black Windsor Hills for fifth grade.

At the start of fourth grade, I attended a predominantly Black school in a lower socioeconomic status area. Most of the kids were cool, though some were rowdy. I was spared from the typical urban school experience because I was placed in the gifted classes. I had caring teachers who were committed to their profession; they were mostly white. When the Triad Program came into effect, however, I switched from the poor school to mostly white Westport Heights and was immediately placed in all of the low reading and math groups. My teacher, Mrs. Thomas, old and white and past retirement age, assumed because I was Black and had joined the class late, I was slow. Mrs. Thomas called me Tina because I told her that was my name in an attempt to avoid the inevitable conversation about how unusual my real name was, and didn't give me another thought. I was bored by the remedial work and longed to take my place among the best and the brightest.

"The teacher placed me in the slow group," I told Ann a few days after starting school.

Ann was not having it. She spoke with Mrs. Thomas, and in no time at all, I moved across the room to join the advanced groups. Getting high grades leveled the playing field between me and my classmates and slowly diminished questions about my family structure. In school, I was a regular kid with both white and Black classmates. In time, everyone understood I was neither an orphan nor adopted. I had two parents and a dog and had to go inside the house when the streetlights came on every evening just like everyone else.

By the time I reached high school, I had found my place among my peers but had dropped my identity as Tina and was insistent on being called Nef. Luckily, our high school added a ninth grade during my first year, so I was spared being called a *scrub* or subjected to a new round of *titty* jokes by the upperclassman. Even so, I was still sensitive about my name and hesitant to reveal it to anyone new. One day, I met a boy on the bus.

"What's your name?"

"Nef."

"Nef, that's it?"

"Neffetiti." It would be a year before I was brave enough to try out the conventional spelling.

He paused for a moment and said, "That's cool."

Suddenly, I liked my full name too. I didn't have to explain that my parents intentionally adjusted the original spelling or that I was named for a queen in Egypt. The really cute guy with eyelashes long enough to touch paid me a compliment. I paid him back with sarcasm. When he told me his name was Everett, I said, "So?" I liked him instantly and spent the next two years running from him.

In another parable of Black adoption, our birth parents became more similar to older siblings or cousins than parents. Ann was the matriarch and pretty much got her way. Even if Diane may have wanted authority over us, she lost her chance when she moved to Texas. We knew this and played on her guilt in the letters we wrote her to get stuff we knew Ann was not going to buy for us. Mainly, we'd ask for designer clothes, and Diane would send cash for reversible Guess jackets, Ton Sur Ton pants, and United Colors of Benetton sweaters. She could act in an advisory capacity and give us things, but she couldn't get us out of punishment.

When I was sixteen years old, I pulled what I thought was a foolproof scheme to go to a dance hall that Ann had forbidden me from going to. My best friend Lori's boyfriend, Claude, and his friend Courtney were going, and I wanted to go too. The plan was for me to spend the night at Lori's, then wait for Courtney and Claude to pick us up and take us dancing. I figured that since I really was going to sleep over at Lori's after the party, a lie by omission seemed reasonable. Ann must have sensed something was up, because after dropping me off, she drove back around the corner. It was like divine choreography—Ann pulled away just as Courtney's burgundy VW Beetle pulled up, with me and Lori piling in. Ann drove by again slowly, and we all froze. I was so busted, but we went anyway. I danced like it was no tomorrow, sweating so hard my pressed hair ballooned into an Afro and burning up in a pink Ton Sur Ton sweatshirt, Guess jeans miniskirt, and low heel white and leopard Doc Martens. The next day, I was served with a two-week *you will not talk on the phone or go anywhere* sentence. My mother did her best to mitigate my punishment by reminding Ann that teens did things like that. Her pleas fell on deaf ears.

It was worth it because I was coming into myself and had even embraced my name Nefertiti, which meant *a beautiful woman walks forth* in full. The name that I used to hate so much now gave me depth, and sometimes I felt like two distinct people. One Nefertiti wore Talbot's preppy suits to speech and debate competitions and mock trials. The other, an Afrocentric teen sporting a white dress and a red, black, green, and yellow sash, wore a Nefertiti medallion hanging from a gold chain. I would recite "Black Panther Seduction," an original creative composition about a black panther whose broken heart left her ferocious and alone in the jungle. I had a mild fixation with the big cat, sensing a depth and vulnerability in her and myself. I even won a couple of awards for my original piece.

Though Ann and Henry had the final say on things, I heard my parents loud and clear when they steered me away from Black Student Union activities when I entered UCLA. Once upon a time, UCLA had been the scene of a massacre in 1969. The unsolved killings of Black Panthers John Huggins and Bunchy Carter were still fresh on their minds nineteen years later. From their time in the Black Power movement, Harold and Diane knew precisely how politically charged and dangerous college campuses could be, and the spell racialized rhetoric could cast on naive freshmen.

Their advice was in line with older people who had seen things. They wanted me to remain focused, and I trusted Diane when she said, "Look, we've already done that bullshit: protesting, chanting, shooting at the police. You don't need to get involved in that."

They needn't have worried. Black students at UCLA in the late 1980s had a more global perspective, with a lot of energy focused on ending Apartheid. Our local concerns involved racial profiling of Black people by the campus police department and who was up on their African history. I was clear on my identity as a Black woman from Windsor Hills and aware that I was a beneficiary of the civil rights movement, 1960s student protests, and the Black Power movement. I was no stranger to supporting my community, having performed community service projects in high school and as a debutante. So, when the seniors found out that my parents were part of the Black Power movement and wanted me to immerse myself in the Black Student Union, I was able to politely decline. My parents and other young people's efforts had allowed me to enjoy my undergraduate years without incident, and I did. I pledged a historically Black sorority, worked on my mentor's legislative campaign, and burned rubber up and down the 405 freeway visiting friends at other UCs or flying to the East Coast to hang on the yard at Howard University.

When I was a senior, I took a political science class: Malcolm X and Black Radical Politics. You would think that with activist parents, I would have aced that class. Well, the professor was a white hippy who was stuck in the seventies. He used to sit cross-legged on the table at the front of the lecture hall and "rap" to the class about Frantz Fanon and liberation struggles throughout the world. Instead of words, he drew squiggles on the white board that I assume must have represented the thinking process or psychology of men like Malcolm X and Ché Guevara. I had no idea what he was talking about. I tried to read *The Wretched of the Earth* but got lost in the small print and hot sands of Algeria. When I had a paper due, I either called my dad or went to see him and told him my situation. He gave me all of the answers, and I earned—well, he earned—a B on my assignment.

Undergraduate flew by, and my early restless confusion about becoming a writer or lawyer was short-lived. Ann and Henry had programmed me to work hard, get a solid education, and go to law school. They, along with my aunt Helen and my uncle Roy, were not on board with my pursuit of the arts, believing I would become a starving artist. Their fears did not deter me. The creativity my dad instilled continued to grow, and I never stopped writing.

I did live like an artist, bouncing from job to job, traveling all over the world and casually dating Black, Iranian, Latino, and white men, although nothing ever really serious developed.

Despite my lack of a husband or a singular career, in my early thirties, I began thinking about potential paths to motherhood. I thought a lot about the way I had been raised—my chaotic early childhood living with Harold and Diane; the uncertainty and pain I felt each time Harold went to jail and when Diane abruptly moved to Texas; the safety and comfort I felt as the center of

Ann and Henry's home after the Black adoption took place and Kareem and I landed there for good. Did I have the potential to be someone's mother? Was I destined to repeat my parents' history? I didn't think so—in fact, I felt in my bones that I was truly meant to have a family.

I came to the realization that Harold and Diane had not been ready to be parents when I was born. They were irresponsible and selfish. They were also brave, passionate, and reckless, and ironically, wanted the same thing their parents wanted: a better life for their children.

If only my parents understood how brave their parents were to ride that wave into the unknown, moving from the segregated South to the west and never looking back. If only my grandparents understood how brave their children were for directly challenging *the man* and standing up to an unjust, racist, sexist world. The only thing separating them was style. How wonderful it would have been if the four of them could have met in the middle. I guess I was the middle, a perfect blend of a free-spirited outlook on life, a love of words, and the strength to take risks. My parents' legacy combined with my grandparents' steady hand, dependability, and selflessness made me strong enough to think I could build a family on my own.

Mommie Dearest, Daddy's Dead

While my dad had always shared his story and beliefs with me, my mother, Diane, was a bit of a mystery. After she moved to Houston, Kareem's and my interactions with her were limited to the Christmas season, a random week or two during the school year, graduations, and two humid weeks in Houston during the summer.

"She doesn't spend a lot of time with us," I once complained to Kareem. She was visiting LA during the holidays but was out and about doing other things most of the time. She may as well have been in Texas. After the initial thrill of her arrival, shopping sprees in high-end Westwood, or an outing to the movies to see horror movies our grandparents would not take us to, Diane was gone. From my preteen perspective, the point of her visit should have been to see us, not her friends. So I resented when she disappeared and then reappeared to take us to Johnny's Pastrami on Adams or Langer's Deli on Alvarado, across from MacArthur

Park, for beef-and-barley soup. I learned to be indifferent and soon girded myself for her visits with the expectation that she would be in and out.

Diane was a fly girl and owned the 80s. Marcus, her common-law husband, had struck gold in street pharmaceuticals, and they lived large with multiple Mercedes-Benz cars, his and hers mink coats, and a nice home in an unassuming subdivision in Houston, Texas. She shared her largesse with us, and our summers in Texas included rafting the Guadalupe River, viewing Houston Astros baseball games, and attending Maze featuring Frankie Beverly concerts. I never questioned my mother's love, but none of the stuff or trips could undo the fact that she lived in another state or that I didn't always feel important to her.

Though we spent time with my father's family, Diane never went with us to see Grandma and Pop when she came to visit, and my dad did not come around when my mother was in town. I'm not sure if he was being respectful of her time with us or if he just wanted to avoid her, but their separation was exacerbated by the fact that she was living the high life in Houston. She smoked cigarettes but had kicked her drug habit, while my dad was still struggling. My mother mailed us photos of the gleaming cars in her driveway, pictures of fun times in Cancun and at Mardi Gras in New Orleans, and one of herself posing in eel skin cowboy boots. The life she presented was carefree and glamorous, but it did not include us.

When she was in Los Angeles, Diane went on the hunt for

expensive perfume and always carried a makeup bag filled with diamonds, gold, silver, and turquoise jewelry.

"Here, I want you to have this." She took a diamond ring off her finger and gave it to me one day when I was sixteen. It was pretty, with three diamonds in a gold floral setting. We were sitting in my bedroom listening to Michael Jackson. I slid it onto my ring finger and watched it dangle. "It's too big."

"Wear it on your middle finger, then," she said, proud of her ability to cast off such an expensive item. We were almost like girlfriends. Almost.

I admired the ring on my finger. In that moment, it was cool. I didn't know many girls my age with diamond rings, so I wore it to school. But the luster quickly wore off. Just as Diane had been unimpressed with her parents' old-fashioned ways and their departure from all that she knew in Compton, I was equally unimpressed with her lifestyle. I accepted whatever gifts she gave, but that did not make her my mama.

Kareem was the only one who understood how I felt. Our mother swung by with presents and good times, but we still longed for a more stable presence from her. Our Black adoption was in place, and I didn't question the lack of discussion that went on about our living situation. As an adult, I realized that culturally Black people did not question the details of a family's dynamic, as long as everything was going well. Only when shit went sideways, like bad grades, talking back, or the time I got suspended from a summer computer class for throwing a lit firecracker at a student who had been bothering me, was everyone brought in the loop. In my family, I don't think it occurred to Ann, Henry, or my mother to have the hard conversation or even ask if we felt adrift emotionally because of our informal situation. Their silence communicated that everything was under control, so we never thought to ask questions like, "How long will we live with Ann and Henry?"

Looking back, a simple conversation from Ann and Henry along the lines of, "We're not sure how long you'll be with us. Maybe a couple of years, maybe forever. Either way, your parents love you, and we're happy to have you," probably would have gone a long way.

Instead, we got nothing. We felt abandoned, and we each manifested that feeling differently. Kareem, who was a great athlete, became a class clown. He was very popular and used humor to mask his pain. I hid my emptiness in my books and began to pull away. Kareem wanted Diane's affection, and I wanted to understand her like I understood our dad. Then Harold was murdered when I was twenty-one, and it was like the universe had played a cruel joke on me. The one person I shared everything with was gone, and I was stuck having to settle for my mother. After years of emotional and physical absence, she tried to step up our relationship. I guess she thought that since my dad was gone, she would fill that space. She started calling multiple times per week, mailed Hallmark cards with sweet sentiments, and made it clear that she was there if I needed anything.

I refused her overtures. I didn't call, and when she came to visit, I saw her only begrudgingly. If we went to dinner, I would sit at the table with little or nothing to say. As usual, my mother would be dressed to the nines with makeup perfectly applied. The more she pushed, the more I resisted. All along, I strongly identified with my grandparents, who had become my parents. They were my heroes. They sacrificed their retirement and money to care for Kareem and me. In comparison, my mother did not seem like a good parent or role model of motherhood.

Maybe if Diane had shared who she was with me, I would have felt differently and been less critical of who I thought she was. I had grown ambivalent about having a relationship with her, and turned my focus to figuring out what I wanted to do for a career—become a lawyer or a writer.

During my first year of law school, I had a revelation. Bored to tears and stressed with the amount of reading and endless debates with classmates over case law and tortfeasor liability, I began writing fiction. Since my high school stab at creative writing, I had written a couple of poems but nothing long form. The oppression of being a law student reignited that old spark to become a writer like my dad. I didn't tell my grandparents. American history had determined that doctor, teacher, or lawyer were safer professions for Black children chasing the American dream. Expectations were high because we were playing catch up from hundreds of years of institutional racism and segregation. Aspirational Black parents, who still had the strength to dream for their children, insisted on these paths. They did not want to see their offspring beat up by life, struggling, or denied opportunities because of their race or gender.

Lynchings of successful Blacks thought to be "uppity" by whites were still clearly in the rearview mirror, and no parent would knowingly put their child in harm's way by encouraging participation in a profession that had a history of negative outcomes. Black parents had witnessed enough violence against Black business owners in Tulsa, New York, Rosewood, and Atlanta to last several lifetimes. Suicide, public humiliation, homelessness, and drug overdoses of artists and musicians whose amazing talents were stifled or stolen by the white establishment made them leery of the arts and other nontraditional fields. The odds of success for Blacks in film, literature, photography, modeling, fine arts, and the culinary arts were marginal compared to whites. So white children got to chase dreams, because, win or lose, the spoils always seemed to go to them. Black parents simply wanted their kids to win, in any way that seemed reasonably attainable.

I had to be surreptitious in resurrecting my dream of being a writer. I kept my room a mess of yellow legal tablets and open law books strewn across my bed. A close-up of my computer monitor, however, would have revealed I was attempting to write a novel. I was writing about love's progression through hell and using poetry to describe heartbreak over a guy I had dated in undergrad. It was so over the top! My characters, Baby and Toe-Up, brought respite from my thoughts of eventually taking the bar exam.

The more I wrote, the more I craved the freedom to create.

I was so weary and conflicted about not wanting to disappoint my grandparents that I developed irritable bowel syndrome. My appetite waned because the gas and acid in stomach set my intestines on fire. The pain was intense, waking me out of my sleep. I would be doubled over in pain, trying not to move a muscle, lest the burning sensation return. I subsisted on Mylanta, salad, cut-and-bake chocolate chip cookies, and hot tea for six months. I lost a lot of weight and looked like a twelve-year-old. I didn't know where to turn or what I was going to do until I found Hermann Hesse's *Siddhartha*. In the pages about the evolution of man's consciousness, I reached an unspoken truth—I did not want to be a lawyer. The writing was on the wall, but family expectations were in place. I kept the charade up through the spring.

That winter break, my mother's fourteen-year relationship with her common-law husband, Marcus, was falling apart, and she wanted to come home to LA, to the place where I had peace, community, and emotional stability.

Her announcement broke me. I had written her a letter in September telling her that she was a dark cloud to my silver lining. I told her that while I could count on her to show up for celebratory events like graduations, she was never there for me on a regular Thursday. I resented her presence and had a hard time faking excitement when she was in town. She wrote back saying she felt like the dark cloud too, and went on to explain what she was going through. Everything was about her. Never an apology for her actions, never an acknowledgment of my feelings, just how bad *she* felt. Her letter infuriated me and further strained our nearly nonexistent relationship.

The night I heard she might leave Marcus, I sat in the middle of my bed, junky with law books, ink pens, and liquid paper, and cried. I had not cried since my father died two years before. Despite everything that had happened in my life, I was generally a happy person, but that night I was distraught. My carefully crafted separate worlds were threatening to collide. I thought how selfish it was of Diane to run home to Ann and Henry when things got hard. They had been bailing Diane out her whole life *and* raised her kids. Wasn't that enough? Why couldn't she move away from Marcus but stay in Houston? I didn't understand why she needed to come back to Los Angeles.

Ann must have sensed something was up. That night, she kept appearing in my bedroom doorway. I would not look up from my book, and the third time she popped in, I was openly crying. She asked what was wrong, and I told her that if Mom came home, I was leaving. I had no job and no money, but I was determined to find my own place if I had to. Ann rocked and shushed me. I had finally adjusted to the years of Diane's absence and needed her to stay in Texas.

When school resumed, I went to the school psychologist. Once again, I was going against the grain, breaking ranks with cultural norms about how Black people handled family drama. White people put all of their business in their street, Black people did not. We'd rather self-medicate with marijuana or alcohol or

sex or shopping or perfection or food or suffer in quiet desperation than bare our soul to strangers, especially white ones. That
was a no-no, but I had nowhere else to turn. That was not me
acting white, it was me trying to untangle my feelings.

"You must be crazy," my mom said over the phone. She had
decided not to leave Marcus after all. And when I spoke with
my busybody aunt Helen later, she warned me, "Don't be telling
white people our business."

"I would've gotten a Black therapist, but that's all the school
had," I defended. "All I'm trying to do is get my head right. What's
so wrong with that?" I needed help finding a place for my mother
in my head and my heart. I already thought of her as an older
sister, but had unresolved feelings about being the daughter of a
woman who left her kids to go live it up in another state.

A few days later, Kareem and I were at home, sitting across
from each other in the kitchen. He was still on winter semester
break. "You're going to make Mom feel bad," he said.

"What about my feelings?" I shot back. "Why am I the bad
guy? You can go to therapy too, you know."

"No way," he said adamantly. His loyalty was torn between
the woman he missed the most and his sister, who had been there
with him through thick and thin.

"Suit yourself." As far as I knew, no one in my family had ever
gone to therapy. No wonder they were giving me the side-eye. In
my next session with Dr. Jamison, she cut right to the chase.

"You have been waiting for your mother to comfort that little girl inside of you, and that is not going to happen," Dr. Jamison said firmly. "You have to do that yourself."

"How?" I was bewildered and saddened that I would be stuck doing my mother's work. Hadn't I already done enough? I took care of my little brother in that cramped Inglewood apartment when she and my dad were too drunk or high to do so. I never told anyone about the time Diane took us to the welfare office on West Boulevard and told us to tell the social worker we were hungry. I was seven, and my parents had split two years before, and she needed more money. Or the next year when we saw our Christmas presents hidden in the closet and as an apology, she made us tell her boyfriend, "I'm sorry, Daddy." We already had a dad, and it wasn't that guy. I hated her for that. I covered for her over and over, and now I had to comfort myself because she still could not do it.

"Start by telling that little girl she is okay. And you are. Your grandmother has been your mother all along."

That made me cry tears of relief. Finally, through all of the family silence, an outsider quickly acknowledged what I had known all along. I had never been without a mother. Ann had been with me, showing up, caring for me, and loving me as a mother loves a daughter. I was now free to claim Ann as my mother. Dr. Jamison's suggestion was priceless. I shared none of this valuable information with my family. They couldn't get past the fact that I was seeing a psychologist, which was fine. Therapy was for my healing, not theirs. Without apology, I was on the emotional mend.

Later that spring, I went to Houston for a law school conference and refused to see my mother while I was there. I spoke to her briefly before the trip and called when I arrived at the hotel, twenty minutes from her home. My friends and I were preparing to go out, and she was pissed that I refused to go to her house. "I already told you I'm not coming to your house, and you're not coming here." I was using the telephone in the bathroom of the hotel suite, with ten of my friends waiting for me to come out.

"Girl, are you okay?" my friend Dana asked from the other side of the door.

I covered the receiver with my hand. "I'm fine. I'll be right out." I was annoyed that Diane expected me to go to her and make nice. We had barely spoken since I went to therapy, and just because I was in town didn't mean I had to act like everything was cool. I was attached to the grudge I held and still processing what I learned in therapy. The little girl inside of me was fragile.

"But I'm your mother," she said.

"That doesn't change anything." I hung up, knowing that one day I would become a mother myself and know exactly what *not* to do.

I got kicked out of law school at the end of that term, having spent more time on myself and writing than my studies. I wasn't upset. The dismissal was my ticket out of a predictable path, and I was free to be me, until I figured out what was next. Though my heart was set on writing full time, I had to eat, and returned to graduate school, where I earned a master's degree in Afro-American studies with an emphasis in United States history and women's studies. School was a day job where I had room to pursue my passion. It was during this period that my writing took off. My old fictional friends, Baby and Toe-Up, became real characters in the first of two novels I published. My books were part of the launch of the Black romance genre in the mid-1990s. It was an exhilarating time and the beginning of my writing career. My family, who had been unsupportive at first, now bragged endlessly about my success. Henry took out ads announcing the publication of my books in Black newspapers the *Los Angeles Wave Newspapers* and the *Los Angeles Sentinel*. He was so proud.

After my first book came out in 1995, my mentor, Marguerite, who was a member of the California state legislature and recipient of a Black adoption by her aunt, threw me a lavish book signing party at the California African American Museum. Henry flew my mother in. On my way to the museum, I stopped by Ann and Henry's. My mother was getting ready and wanted to ride with me. Before we left, she did what she always did—made everything about her.

"So, you didn't want me to come," she said, sliding on black pantyhose. She was sitting on the toilet lid in the small bathroom, and I was standing in the doorway.

"I never said that." I rolled my eyes and crossed my arms. "Can I have one day about me?"

"You don't act happy that I'm here."

I'd had enough. "You should ride with Ann and Henry," I said. I told Ann I would meet them at the venue, jumped in my two-seater Honda, and left.

Standing before the microphone in front of 150 people, I thanked and acknowledged almost everyone in the wide-open space, except my mother. I forgot she was there. As I left the mic, Marguerite whispered, "Your mother. Say something."

"Oops," I said and ran back to the podium. "Oh, and thanks to my mom who came out from Texas." I gave her an awkward hug and everyone applauded.

My relationship with my mother seemed to be completely stuck. We couldn't get past the stalemate.

Decision Made

I knew the exact moment I wanted to become a mother. It was September 2006, and I was thirty-six years old. I had just moved into my small apartment in Beverly Hills with my two dogs, LL Cool J and Sunday Morning. I made the most out of the dull tan walls by adding a hand-painted bamboo curtain of Frida Kahlo to separate the hall from the living room. I converted the dining area into my office and spent many days seated at my powder-blue desk typing away on a laptop. I had four bookcases packed with books, hundreds of CDs, two black velvet couches, and an itty-bitty television perched on top of a copy of the *Complete Works of William Shakespeare*. My bedroom contained a painting of Elmina Slave Castle, a framed poster of the cover of my first book, and my most prized possession, a mounted poster of Prince during his *Purple Rain* days.

Of course, my family clowned my apartment. My grandparents still lived in our Windsor Hills house, and now they looked at my hovel sideways. They could not understand how a woman with a master's degree from UCLA refused to be further along in life. I had classmates who grew up to produce the *Barbershop* franchise and *Chappelle's Show*, win Emmys and Grammys, get drafted for the NFL, own restaurants, and climb to the top of their professional game. While Ann and Henry never compared me to anyone, at least not to my face, I knew their dream for me had not been to become the free-spirited bourgeoisie Bohemian I was now. However, two published novels and coveted spots at prestigious writers' conferences later, I had made my dream come true, proving to everyone that my meandering path through life was working.

Lori, my childhood best friend, was an adoptee and licensed clinical social worker in adoptions, who had become a mom a few years before, and named me godmother to her son. My brother had become a father, and all of the children on the periphery of my life set off teeny-tiny stirrings of motherhood. I thought I would make a good mother. I was fun, had a lot of energy, and had good parenting examples from both sets of grandparents. Then, one day the stirrings of motherhood turned into what I called the full-fledged *mommie-jones*, an overwhelming desire to be a mother that crept into my spirit and would not turn me loose.

Suddenly, I noticed every stroller, bib, car seat, diaper bag, crib, and onesie ever made in the entire world. I began reading reviews of baby products, researched ways to introduce babies to pets, and thought up names for my future child. I imagined decorating a nursery, kissing the bottom of little feet, and dancing the "Hokey Pokey." I had a *love hangover* and didn't want a cure.

Plain and simple, I decided I wanted to adopt a baby. I had been so blessed to have amazing grandparents who modeled how to love and provide for children they did not birth. I revered traditional paths to motherhood via marriage but was leery of the struggles my friends had endured through the early years of their partnerships. Some even divorced, and I didn't want any part of that.

I had a lot of opinions about marriage, and most of them were wrong. Ann and Henry had gotten together relatively quickly after meeting. Therefore, I assumed that people met, agreed to be together, got married, and lived happily ever after, because Ann, Henry, and my father's parents all made relationships look easy. By the time I came along, my grandparents were two or more decades into their marriages. Whatever kinks they experienced had been ironed out long ago. I never saw the negotiation process or how my grandmothers dealt with disappointment and conflict with their husbands.

While they once functioned more traditionally during my mother's upbringing, my maternal grandparents became egalitarian when it came to housework. Henry took care of outside the house and he grocery shopped, washed dishes, cooked his own meals, schlepped me and Kareem back and forth to school and extracurricular activities, did his own laundry, and paid most of the bills. My grandmother cooked for us, took us clothes shopping, and paid her share of the household bills.

My grandfathers, however, threw a wrench into my fairy-tale idea of marriage. They had strong opinions on "young men today" and didn't hesitate to share them. Henry's sage dating advice was: "Get yourself a good education, get married, and have a family." Pop followed Henry with: "These young men ain't what they used to be. You have to be able to take care of yourself." They were trying to protect me and my female cousins.

Not done with dating, I started categorizing men into two groups: potential sperm donor or not. I began to worry that in my haste to become a mother, my relationship discernment antennae would be off-kilter. Sure enough, they were. The guys I liked were just like me: emotionally unavailable, skittish, scared of being vulnerable, and invested in being right. I dated a series of peacocks, who looked good on paper but were either too fast, too unreliable, or too not into me. Though they were all high achievers and came from good homes, I got in more pickles thinking I could emotionally support them. They were the devil I knew, because Henry was non-affectionate and emotionally unavailable. Pop, on the other hand, was loving, and I enjoyed his attention, but he was not the primary male influence in my life. I was chasing my elusive, irrepressible, warm-and-fuzzy father, but expecting men to behave like my dependable grandfather. That foolishness allowed me to focus on my writing and how to get out of working a nine-to-five job, but prevented me from investing time in meaningful relationships. I was willing to have relations but not relationships, and slow to take responsibility when those unions did not pan out. Despite all of the relationship books I read on how and when to play it cool, when to have sex, and what to wear, I was floundering. I kept picking the same type of man over and over, thinking life could be *Love Jones*, *The Best Man*, *Love & Basketball*, *Brown Sugar*, and every other Black romance movie ever made. I used to purchase *The Knot* magazine and cut pictures of wedding dresses out and paste them to my vision board. My beau and I would dance to "Love Ballad" and make beautiful babies. I was longing for roses, marriage, and chocolate, but wanted it without all the drama intimacy could bring. While I suspected there were great guys out there, I agonized that I'd choose one with an inferior gene pool or waste time attached to a fool I couldn't stand. Then we would divorce. Having spun that scenario in my mind hundreds of times, I chose the less emotional messy route. I saved my most authentic self for the trees I was killing by writing, printing, and shredding drafts of a novel I had workshopped during writer's conferences, tabling my desire to become a mother via marriage.

Adoption was still an option. The seeds of choosing it had been planted in my mind years before, and I was leaning into making that a reality. I figured my decision would raise eyebrows in the Black community because we typically adopted relatives. Having a connection, even a tenuous one, was culturally more acceptable than blindly accepting a child we knew nothing about. We were also loathe to involve the system in our evaluation of who needed a mother, because we loved our mamas, no matter how trifling, strung out, mean, or absent. We might talk bad about someone, but we didn't want the system to publicly deem her unfit to take care of her own kids.

In my case, there were no available children in my immediate or extended family to adopt, so I would be taking in a child I did not know. That would mean breaking code and acting like white people, whose adoption experiences were already normalized in the eyes of whites and Blacks. They could adopt a child from anywhere and no one blinked. My community was still warming up to that idea.

In the midst of my dating foibles, the idea that I could become an adoptive mother was tested. I worked with a woman who sponsored a South African toddler infected with HIV. Though the orphan remained in Johannesburg, Janet sent money and even visited her. The pictures of her baby were beautiful and haunting. I immediately signed up to sponsor two children. I sent clothing and a monthly nominal allowance until their mother took them home. Free-spirited me was so moved that I could help these orphans that I became officially open to the idea of adopting as my first choice in becoming a parent. Having watched all of the red tape Janet experienced trying to bring baby Massa to the States, I decided to look closer to home.

It took some doing, but that summer I managed to reconcile my artistic and emotional selves and asked myself why what I had wasn't enough. Why wasn't I satisfied? I had two wonderful nieces and a godson that I doted on. Time spent with them was all fun and no responsibility. I answered to no one, came and went as I pleased. I bought a fancy MINI Cooper, rocked a super-cute pixie haircut, and had a closet filled with stylish clothes. Life was good, but boring. The one thing I wanted more than anything required absolute honesty with myself. I did not want to submit to a man's idea of who I should be or which career path I should take. I liked operating on my own schedule, beholden to no one. This was a recipe for me to remain single, and I was fine with that. I might not have known what I wanted in a husband, but what I did know was that I wanted to adopt a baby.

Mommy Lessons

I called Lori at home. "Hey there, guess what?"

"What now, fool?" She was laughing already.

"I'm ready," I said coyly.

"To?"

I paused. "Adopt."

"That's great news!" she exclaimed. "You'll make a great mother."

"You think so?" Her approval meant a lot. We had been friends since kindergarten and had teamed up for countless (mis) adventures. We knew each other's secrets, supported each other through success, failure, heartbreak, marriage, and now mother-hood. She was my oldest and dearest friend, the closest thing I had to a real sister. I loved her immensely. On top of that, she was the resident expert on adoption. If I could trust anyone to green-light my decision to adopt, it would be her.

"Just so you know, in California, you have to foster first."

"What does that mean?"

"Anyone who wants to adopt has to be a foster parent first. It's to make sure you really, really, really know what you're getting into."

"Whoa." That stopped me short.

"Yeah, our state is into family reunification. We want to give birth parents a chance to raise their kids. If that doesn't work out, foster parents become adoptive parents. Other states have different rules."

"That's fine. How do I begin?" Once my mind was made up about something, I wasn't one to delay.

"Go online to the From the Heart website and sign up for the orientation. I'll call you when I get to work tomorrow and tell you when the next PS-MAPP training is."

"Cool, thanks."

"One last thing, because of our relationship, I can't be your social worker."

"That sucks." I was disappointed—having Lori walk me through the process would have made it feel much less intimidating.

"It's a conflict of interest. I'll hook you up with Donna. She's one of the best."

In her work as an adoption social worker, Lori assisted prospective adoptive families, foster children, and biological parents to navigate the sometimes-misaligned policies that dictated how the foster care system operated. She was the one who clued me in on how Black boys were least likely to be adopted. It was assumed that Black boys had behavior issues and were harder to control. Because of this first assumption, when these boys became men, they were labeled hypermasculine. Patrick Derilus writes in *Sometimes I Cry: The Toxic Hypermasculinity of Black Men* that "this construct, created by white patriarchy, exaggerated black men as over-domineering, super-powered, callous, deranged, insensitive, and animalistic brutes. Forced to live under laws written and enacted by white men to contain this threat, we were all indoctrinated with fear of Black men." That was why Black boys were least likely to be adopted. Girls, on the other hand, were seen as sweet and cuddly. I didn't like that Black boys were discriminated against and decided to adopt a Black boy. The whole notion of an entire group of little boys being left behind awakened my Black Power roots. Adopting a baby boy would allow me to lift as I climbed.

When I decided to adopt, I viewed adoption in terms of who wanted kids and who did not. Most of my friends who had children were married and had limited interactions with Black or white traditional adoptive parents. I knew a little about foster care, having spent a short time as a kindergarten and first grade teacher in the late 1990s at an elementary school in a poor Black and Latino neighborhood. About one-third of my twenty first graders were foster children. Some were better off than others. One particular child, Ontray, would start the week off clean and be dirty by midweek. His foster mother had several children she cared for and was overwhelmed trying to keep up with all of them. Ontray was teased about his filthy clothes and his status as a ward of the state.

Another little boy, TJ, used to bring debit cards from the women's jail where his mother was housed for show and tell. He told us that he used them to buy soda or candy during their visits. TJ lived with his younger brother, grandmother, and uncle, because his father was also incarcerated. It was clear that his grandma was not pleased with this arrangement, and she had no plans to informally or formally adopt TJ and his brother. She was mean to everyone, and TJ used to cut up in class. The teachers labeled him a problem. In fact, before I even met TJ, another kindergarten teacher, Ashley, tried to warn me about him.

"He constantly disrupts class." Ashley shook her blond curls. "No one can do anything with him." She meant well, but her unconscious bias against Black boys blinded her from even trying to figure out the best way to teach him.

"Thanks, Ashley, I'll see what I can do." I had no training, no child psychology or teacher practicum courses under my belt. What I did have was compassion and a sneaking suspicion that the *problem child* just missed his mother. As the school year progressed and TJ's dad reentered his life, his grades and attitude greatly improved. In that neighborhood, foster care was the norm, requiring other adults to step up and be more open-minded about how to support those children. I quickly adjusted to family configurations of biological and nonbiological siblings living under the same roof or down the street from one another. I witnessed their little lives enhanced or destroyed by foster care and wished I could take them all home.

Now, my only mission was to become a mom, in the fastest and most efficient way possible. Private adoption was too unpredictable and expensive, and international adoption seemed unnecessary in a county with more than thirty thousand children already waiting for a home. My own backyard was a great place to grow my family, and adoption through the Los Angeles Department of Children and Family Services (DCFS) a.k.a. the County seemed like a no-brainer. I attended an orientation and signed up for DCFS's Permanency and Safety: Model Approach to Partnership and Parenting Training (PS-MAPP). DCFS was an inclusive agency that welcomed anyone interested in becoming a foster/adoptive parent, regardless of race, ethnicity, sexual orientation, or marital status. Their mission was to prepare families to provide stable homes for children who could not return to their biological families. Training was held at a California community college, and I drove nineteen miles from Beverly Hills to a suburb south of Los Angeles for six consecutive Saturdays.

On the first day of training, I woke up at five in the morning, entirely too early for a nine o'clock class. My dogs were stretched out on their bed like, *what's wrong with this chick?* I tossed and turned and finally got up. Part of my anxiety was over what to wear, because I wanted to look like the type of mother that I wanted to be. I faced the closet and pulled out five different outfits ranging from business, to business casual, to walk-the-dogs casual. I settled on faded jeans, a pink shirt, and flats. Traffic was light, and I jammed along to Prince's "Little Red Corvette," trying to sing my nerves away.

Apart from Lori and my cousin Kisha, I had told only a few friends who I knew would be supportive of my plans that I was going to start the training. My family was on a need-to-know basis only, because I knew they would probably not be thrilled about my plans. I had every right to adopt and would find every resource to make it happen. Nothing was going to stop me.

As I approached the freeway exit, I wondered if I would be the only single person in the room, or the only Black single woman in the room. That question was answered shortly after I arrived at the classroom where the training would be held. The college chair desks were arranged in a U-shape facing a white board. At each seat sat a pencil basket, yellow sticky notes, fluorescent highlighters, a three-ring binder, and a box of tissue was off to the side. Today, twenty-three prospective foster/adoptive parents with varying degrees of experience with foster children would spend time bonding and learning about adoption and the foster care system.

During the class introductions, I met Charmaine, another single woman, and my nerves settled down. We were joined by several married couples, a couple in their late fifties, and an empty nester whose adult children weren't pleased with her decision to adopt. A few of the families already had foster children living with them and needed to get licensed by the County and state of California to adopt. One couple was infertile. Racially, we were a motley crew of predominantly Black people, one white couple, and two Latinx families.

In this setting, I was not special. No one raised their eyebrows when I shared the details of my Black adoptive childhood; no one blinked when I shared that drug abuse tore my parent's marriage apart or that I wanted to adopt a Black baby boy. I was in the right place, and the butterflies that woke me that morning were soon gone.

All PS-MAPP trainings were led by a group of three people: a social worker with a master's degree in social work (MSW), a certified foster/adoptive trainer, and a resource parent. Our trio, Donna, Latrece, and Stephanie had the awesome task of educating prospective caregivers about DCFS, the overall foster care system, how children entered the system, who was eligible to foster or adopt, the difference between fostering and adopt-ing, and why biological parents surrendered or lost their children. This was priceless information, and the more I learned, the more my assumptions and beliefs about parents, mothers in particular, who abandoned their children, were disrupted.

The first day of training became my reckoning with my judgment of my own unfit and absent mother. I had a limited understanding of how birth parents felt and tended to empathize with the children who had been abandoned because I had been one of them. I had no empathy for parents who left their children for someone else to feed, clothe, and comfort. I knew the toll that drug addiction took on children and the spiral of neglect it created, making kids chronically absent from school and unable to articulate why Mom or Dad had not fed them. I remember being heartbroken but remaining loyal and protective of my parents, who gave me life but did not show up when I needed them. And I knew the embarrassment of going back and forth to Grandma's, because my parents, who swore they would die for me, couldn't sit still long enough to make a home we could share. In order to become the mother I wanted to be, I had to develop true compassion for the parents I'd had.

Fortunately, the parenting classes helped me understand that most biological parents were themselves victims of child abuse, neglect, the foster care system, drug addiction, homelessness, youth, mental health issues, or incarceration, and would do better for their children if they could. Latrece, the adoption trainer, drove this point home on more than one occasion. Biological parents who surrendered their kids or had them taken from them more than likely spent their own childhoods in the system and never learned how to take care of themselves. They looked for love in all the wrong places and immaturely thought having a baby would make up for the abandonment they experienced as a child. They were human beings whose lives had come undone because of institutional racism, poverty, criminalization, race, gender, and poor choices. Becoming a mother through adoption was no longer about me, but about developing sympathy for the Dianes of the world.

My developing understanding of these birth parents revealed a startling connection: If we judge the parents for their shortcomings, we are actively judging the very children we want to serve. Even if we never directly say "your father is a jailbird," our negative energy might imply that the little boy is lucky to have been removed from his family and put into more reliable hands. I knew this all too well, having deflected questions about my missing-in-action parents, and I was determined not to pass this type of judgment on to my own child. I also learned that thoughts are powerful and can cause us to unconsciously act different toward a child we adopted or fostered. We may be harder on them or make excuses for inappropriate behavior. Either result is detrimental to the child, who is already dealing with loss, low self-esteem, and grief. Our job as foster parents is not to add insult to injury, but to provide a safe, supportive environment for the kids and their biological parents, who are trying to reunify with them.

DCFS held multiple contracts with agencies that offered parenting classes and domestic violence and sexual assault support groups for women whose children were detained by social workers and placed into foster care. These classes were a bridge toward family reunification. If the mother or father demonstrated stability and an ability to parent, then the County returned the children. Of course, life for these women and men frequently got in the way, and we prospective foster/adoptive parents would be at the ready should the need arise.

I soon realized this process was not for everyone, and the preparation was challenging. There were many layers of bureaucracy between attending that first class and finally getting matched with a child. In order to get licensed to foster by the state of California,

I would have to complete the **PS-MAPP** training; clear criminal background and fingerprint checks at the state and national level; earn a pediatric first aid certificate; obtain confidential letters of recommendation from friends or associates; pass a physical exam with written proof from a physician; submit to an inspection of my home; obtain up-to-date shot records for my two dogs; and complete a home study, which examined my relationship with my brother, dating life, employment history, and a list of my support system. I underwent an emotional and mental health assessment by my social worker Donna and had to demonstrate my ability to financially, physically, and emotionally be a forever family. I even had to disclose all the details of my own Black adoption by Ann and Henry. I was honest but kept the description of my child-hood short and sweet. Lori warned me not to sugarcoat anything about my past. The agreement I was entering into was not the TV version of adoption. This was not the informal adoption that I experienced as a child. This was legal.

It was a lot.

The paperwork was not difficult to complete. I had completed enough job, literary scholarship, and residency applications in my lifetime to kill a small tree. From my academic and professional training, I knew how to prioritize tasks and meet deadlines. And, most importantly, I was determined to see it through.

As I went through the long process, I was hyperaware of the poor image DCFS and DCSS (Department of Child Support Services) had in the community. The behemoth agencies were known for being unable to retain top leadership, tolerating criminally negligent social workers, and enabling sadistic foster parents who maimed or killed foster children. There had been numerous reports of children being lost in the system and forced to languish in foster care for years where they were starved, burned, sexually molested, and suffered unspeakable acts of cruelty. The news reports that seemed to pop up weekly reminded me of Antwone Fisher's memoir *Finding Fish*, which recounted his horrific childhood in foster care in Cleveland during the 1970s.

Accused foster parents graced the front pages with a laundry list of crimes committed against the youth in their care. When the public demanded an explanation, the answer was almost always the same: The child's social worker had not visited regularly or the neighbors had called the child abuse hotline but the allegations of abuse went unsubstantiated. Foster mothers in Los Angeles County tended to be Black women, and the media reinforced the image of the scheming Black welfare mother who preyed on poor and neglected children to get out of working a real job. On the other end of the spectrum were feature stories covering the devoutly white Christian couples who took in every child on the block.

Now that I was on the path to adoption, these stories irritated me. I was particularly annoyed that Black foster mothers were painted in large, ugly brush strokes while the whites-as-saviors-of-Black-children narrative reigned supreme. All of the feel-good movies with white foster mothers like *Losing Isaiah* were warm, loving, and devoted to the Black child they were saving, while the

Black mothers shown in the media were crackheads or some other form of trash straight out of the Black-woman-stereotype guide. I was determined that as soon as I finished the training, I would become a different kind of example of a Black foster mom.

We covered a different topic each week in the PS-MAPP classes. After the first week of introductions and conversation about the challenges birth parents faced, we examined the responsibilities of foster/adoptive parents in the second week. In California, family reunification was the ultimate objective. Whenever possible, children should be with their parents, and to achieve that goal, foster parents had to partner with birth parents and social workers. I understood the spirit of the rule, remembering my own childhood dreams of living with both of my parents, but the mandate felt counterintuitive. I was there to adopt, not engage in a tug-of-war with birth parents who had lost their children. I seriously wondered if I could be a revolving door for kids in need of temporary care. Was I strong enough to let go of a child I had grown to love? I admired foster parents who cared for kids until they found a permanent home, but I was not that generous. I wanted to build a forever family.

Small groups and role-play were the main tools the trainers used to teach us about birth parent-foster parent interactions, appropriate discipline techniques, and how to handle older children who were oppositionally defiant toward authority, fought at school, ran away from home, or acted out sexually. Donna stressed that some foster children intentionally sabotaged their placements in hopes of returning to their biological families. We were instructed not to take negative behavior personally and consider how scary life would have been without our parents, no matter how imperfect they were. Thinking back on the security of knowing that Ann and Henry were always with me and my brother, I began to understand why a child who lived in multiple foster homes would behave in extreme ways to go home or avoid being rejected yet again.

Week three provided information about services available to children and families…and then came the reality check. If any one of us wanted to adopt a newborn, we would be in for a long, long, long wait. Newborns were notoriously hard to find. Even if a mother surrendered her baby or the County detained a child in the hospital after birth, a relative normally stepped forward to take the child. The wait was five, maybe ten, years for Caucasian or Asian babies. Toddlers, sibling sets, and children of color, including biracial children, were more plentiful.

Luckily, the news about tiny babies being hard to come by wasn't devastating for me. Newborns scared me. Their scaly skin and unfocused eyes gave me the willies. I knew if I were to get a newborn, I would be petrified that he would die from Sudden Infant Death Syndrome (SIDS). Ideally, I wanted an older baby who could do tricks like roll over, sit up, and hold his own bottle— old enough to be out of the scary danger zone, but not so old that he would already have picked up traits and habits from whoever was raising him before me. My desires aside, I realized I might have to compromise on the age of the child I wanted to adopt. Telling Donna at this juncture that I only wanted to adopt an infant seemed selfish and ridiculous. I was either going to be all in, or not in at all.

Another challenge I had to face was the fact that, because family reunification was the endgame of fostering, placement disruptions happened all the time. Until a judge legally terminated the biological parents' parental rights, foster parents were supposed to be emotionally prepared to return a foster child to his or her family. A cold truth washed over the group. Here, some of us were preparing our hearts, minds, and pocketbooks for a family, and simultaneously being advised that the child could be taken away at a moment's notice. In other words, there were no guaranteed placements, and we had to agree to be vulnerable shepherds to the whims of children's court, child advocates, and social workers whose job it was to support the reunion of biological parents and their children.

We received a mountain of documents that would eventually serve as the foundation of our family assessment/home study, which included questions about our personal history, lifestyle, parenting experience, psychological profile, strengths and skills in meeting a child's needs, and what our support system looked like. There was no defined minimum income requirement, but we had to demonstrate we could afford to have a child. There was also a strong emphasis on who would be there to help with day care, school pickups, doctor's appointments, illness, and emergencies. For about five minutes, I felt smug. Many couples who got pregnant did not consider those scenarios until it was too late. I was ahead of the game. But before I popped my collar, I had a vision of my future. Who *would* help with pickup? Who would I list as my in-case-of-emergency contact? Where would my child go to school? There weren't actually any simple answers.

I had naively assumed it would be easy to find childcare for my future baby. The timeline of when a child would be placed with me was six months to two years, but I would be up shit's creek if the foster/adoption process moved faster than expected. I was commuting between two college campuses in opposite directions, teaching day and night U.S. history classes, and working a part-time job in communications for a nonprofit. Even though I probably wouldn't meet him for several months, I needed to figure out where my future child would stay while I was working—fast.

I got in touch with Nancy, the owner of an in-home day care not far from where I lived, who came highly recommended by two different friends. Nancy was the proud mother of four adult children, six grandchildren, and one great-granddaughter and had been a childcare provider for thirty years. There were six kids in her care, including an Asian girl who had been transracially adopted by a white woman. Nancy was also adopted herself, having been left on the doorstep of a Catholic orphanage when she was an infant. Her birth mother was white and her birth father was Black, and she was raised in Philadelphia. I couldn't have found a more perfect caregiver for my child.

Since my grandmother was now in her eighth decade of life and fuzzy on details from her early days as a mom in the 1950s, Nancy became my mentor. I needed an older, wiser parenting sounding board and, unbeknownst to Nancy, she had inherited the baton from Ann to provide me with valuable insight on mothering. Elated by the ease of connecting with her, I scratched childcare off my to-do list, only to learn that Nancy was fully booked and couldn't take any more children. She told me to check back in a few months. I picked my face up off the floor and marked my calendar to circle back to her in March.

By the fourth week of training, only fourteen of the original twenty-three in the group remained. Families dropped out or were asked to leave after failing background checks. During the fourth session, we were told that our official status would be simultaneous foster/adoptive parent, meaning we would be foster parents first and then adoptive parents, if the child was available. The distinction was important because only a family court judge had the power to decree a child free to be adopted. During this uncertain time frame, foster parents waited. We waited for family reunification to result in a placement disruption, or the termination of biological parental rights. We waited for social workers to deem us stable enough to parent foster children. We waited for paperwork to be processed at the state and county levels. We held our breath, hoping nothing would delay our voluminous applications.

The path to becoming a mother seemed to stretch on forever, and I understood why Black folks often bypassed this portion of the program in favor of Black adoption. I could have saved myself a lot of trouble and just gotten knocked up. But the urge to become a parent through adoption gave me the patience to endure all the bureaucracy. I used this time to learn an online teaching platform to open up my career options. There was no easy way to get to one of the campuses I worked at, and the department chair kept assigning me classes during the middle of the day. Ninety minutes going to and from work interfered with my other part-time job, and on top of that I was reworking a novel. My third novel had been passed over for publication and Jason, my agent, pulled the fourth one apart. He said I had two books in one and needed to pick one story and work on completing it. That was not exactly what I wanted to hear, but it gave me something to focus on while I got licensed to adopt.

We prospective parents were taught that if we endured all of the red tape, the pot of gold at the end of the rainbow was National Adoption Day, held on the Saturday before Thanksgiving all over the country. Thousands of children and foster parents went before family court judges to be sworn in as a forever family. The County provided free adoption attorneys for National Adoption Day, but families who did not want to wait could have a private ceremony as soon as they received a court date for adoption finalization.

By week five, we were exhausted by PS-MAPP training, but this was the last full class. Once again, the focus would be on foster children—but this time, crack took center stage. In the Black community, this was an extra stigma that delayed the adoption of children in the system. It was such a huge issue, DCFS added it to the curriculum and saved this heavy topic for the end.

Latrece began the discussion. "Crack is the cheap cousin of cocaine. This drug decimated poor communities of color all over the country throughout the 1980s and 1990s. Most people think that kids born to mothers addicted to crack will be intellectually and developmentally delayed, unable to form attachments or assimilate into society."

Stephanie, reading from a manual, chimed in. "Projections that children born to mothers addicted to crack would be doomed to a life of uncertain suffering, of probable deviance and permanent inferiority were scare tactics created by the media to sell newspapers."

Two of the people in our group, Earlene and Sam, "sho'-nuffed." They were an older Black couple who had fostered at least fifty children. They enrolled in PS-MAPP training to adopt a nephew who was in the system. If they didn't go the formal route, he could live with them but would retain foster child status until he turned eighteen, and they wanted to provide a permanent home for him. Earlene raised her hand. "I have seen some of these babies come out the womb with the shakes. With a lot of love and the blood of the lamb, we saw them healed and out playing with the other kids. You can't even tell the difference. I'm not saying the effects of drugs on babies in utero are not devastating, because they are. It's just that crack is not the life sentence everyone thought it was."

"Earlene brings up a good point," Donna interjected. "Early intervention is often the best way to get kids back on track."

I thought of the pejorative headlines that topped the news cycle with visuals of staggering, emaciated men and women, and tales of uncontrolled crime in the hardest hit areas of Los Angeles, Detroit, and New York. Headlines like, "Childhood's End: What Life Is Like for Crack Babies," "Crack's Toll Among Babies: A Joyless View," and "Studies: Future Bleak for Crack Babies" made it easy to dismiss a generation already combatting poverty, incarceration, unemployment, and violence. The *crack baby* label was used indiscriminately to describe many Black children and led to sweeping generalizations and negative stereotypes.

Donna took the next section. "Raise your hand if you think kids born exposed to crack are worse off than those with mothers who were alcoholics."

Most everyone, including me, raised their hands.

"Wrong. Alcohol has irreversible effects upon babies in the womb. So-called *crack babies* parented in chaotic environments by drug addicted parents sometimes fulfill that prophecy and repeat the cycle. However, studies show that by age four, drug addicted/exposed babies who were reared in a loving, stable environment where they were appropriately stimulated, had no difference in their development from non-drug addicted/exposed children raised in a similar setting. That's where you come in."

"Your home," Stephanie said, as she pointed at each of us, "will make the difference for babies with attachment issues, neglected children, and those with delays. Your home will be a nurturing environment that will save a child's life."

They were proposing that, more so than the circumstances of their birth, kids were a product of their environment. There was truth to that, but I knew even kids raised under the best circumstances went off the grid. My parents sure did.

"If a child placed with you needs educational, medical, psychiatric, or psychological services because of drugs or any other reason, DCFS provides these services for free until he turns twenty-one years old. Full medical benefits for minors until he or she is eighteen years old, childcare in some instances, access to support groups, and a small monthly stipend are given to each foster family," Latrece said. "And, Women, Infants, and Children (WIC) for milk, formula, fruits, vegetables, and grains, and post-adoption support is available." It was nice to know that DCFS didn't just place foster kids with new parents and then turn them loose in the world.

We broke for lunch and returned to discuss cultural competency.

Donna ran point. "Before we let you go, we're going to cover transracial foster/adoption placements. DCFS does not discriminate and seeks placements for children for all licensed families."

"Being culturally competent means that you must educate yourself on your child, especially if he or she comes from a different race, ethnicity, or religion than your own. For example, Black people know that Black girls with pressed, chemically straightened, or permed hair do not go swimming right after getting their hair done. But white or Latinx or Asian parents may not. There are things like that that are important to know for every race and identity."

All of the Black women in the room snickered. I was happy that this issue was important enough to be part of the training curriculum. People thought they could just take any baby and never consider culture as an integral aspect of their child's life. Transracially adoptive parents needed to be willing to engage in the hard work of truly getting to know their child. That rule applied to anybody who adopted a child of a different race.

"There are all kinds of books and publications like *Adoptive Families* magazine with articles about cultural traditions like quinceañeras. These are not just random activities, they are necessary aspects of your child's identity and important to their self-esteem."

"We know we threw a lot at you today. This is a decision that should not be made lightly, and it's perfectly okay if you decide not to move forward with foster care or adoption," Latrece said.

After all of that, I was even more determined to make a difference in the life of a little Black boy. I turned my tassel. I was ready to graduate to motherhood.

Awed by the insight I had gained about myself and the foster care system, I spent the next five days getting my house in order. For the first time, I was looking at my home as a mother, instead of a single person. I slid my queen-sized bed over to accommodate a wooden crib, donated by a friend whose child had outgrown it. I bought a diaper caddy that also stored wipes, baby powder, lotion, and diaper rash ointment. I got a small bottle of Johnson's baby shampoo, conditioner kit, baby Motrin, and a first aid kit. I had purchased these items for my nieces before but experienced a weird out-of-body sensation buying them for my future child. I was really doing it. I was going to be somebody's mommy.

It was early in 2007, and I assumed it would be months before I got matched with a child, but I decided to be proactive. I baby-proofed the pointy ends of my entertainment center, looped plastic zip ties through cabinet handles, covered doorknobs with breakaway features, and locked the toilet lid down with a contraption that made it hard for me to open. I bought bottles in various sizes, placed plugs for the television, DVD player, and cable box into a power strip safety container, and then sat on the floor to take in the world from my future son's eye level.

"Oh shit, he could get his fingers stuck in this slot," I said out loud. I went back to Target and got a plexiglass shield for the buttons on the receiver and CD player, and Velcro to anchor my thirty-six-inch television so it couldn't move. I asked my good friend Rudy to latch my overfilled book case to the wall. I would die if it toppled over onto a toddler who was flexing his muscles trying to stand. I posted emergency numbers for the police, poison control, an ambulance company, the fire department, and

Nancy's day care on the cabinet in the kitchen. A space at day care would open in July, and Nancy had agreed to hold a place for us. I chose a pastel jungle theme for the crib and placed the fitted sheet decorated with lions, giraffes, and zebras over the mattress. I propped a large fire-engine–red teddy bear in the corner and thought: *There, I am ready to receive my baby.* My apartment was ready; my mind, not so much. I thought it would be months—maybe years—before I would actually meet my child and returned to my pre-PS-MAPP life.

The spring semester was in full swing, and I was just living life and minding my own business when Donna called six weeks later. "I found a match."

Other People's Fears

During the phone call to discuss the particulars, Donna and I planned to meet up a few days later to discuss the match. I was giddy with anticipation, but then the reality hit. I needed to tell my family what I was up to. While I was 100 percent certain of my ability to love a child who had had less than a stellar start in life, I knew my conservative family might take issue with my decision. Knowing they would worry, I intentionally waited until after I got licensed to foster to share my good news. I wasn't seeking permission, just giving them a heads-up that when I came through the door with a baby, he would be mine and not some child I snatched from the mall. I had already told my cousins Kisha and Nikki of my plans to adopt, and they, like my friends, were excited and supportive. Nikki, who lived in South Carolina, was in the midst of her own private adoption. She had been inspired to adopt by a church member she admired and also wanted a baby boy. We held hands long distance and sojourned together.

I drove to Ann and Henry's a couple of days after I got news of the match. I practiced my speech in my MINI Cooper on the twenty-minute ride over. I didn't warn them I was coming; I did what I always did and showed up. As usual, I was hit with a blast of heat as soon as I stepped into the house. Ann was sitting at the kitchen table watching CNN, and Henry was in his office, just like when I was a little girl. Much like every day of my childhood, collard greens had already been prepared, and Ann was waiting on the cornbread to finish baking. The kitchen had undergone a makeover in the 1990s, when she swapped out the orange cabinets for maple wood and pulled up the runners in the dining room and replaced them with small rose rugs to protect the thick rose pile carpet that lay throughout the house.

I joined Ann at the table. "You want something to eat?" She moved to fix me a plate.

I put my hand over hers. "No, I'm not hungry." I dove right into my announcement. "I'm going to adopt a baby."

Surprised, Ann leaned back in her chair and yelled, "Henry!" To me she asked, "Where are you going to get a baby?"

"The foster care system," I answered matter-of-factly. "Lori is helping me."

Ann stared at me. Henry came into the kitchen, annoyed that he had to stop what he was doing. "What is going on? Ann, why are you yelling?"

"Tell Henry what you just said." The look of shock cleared from her face, leaving behind recognition. She knew me. I had already refused to become a lawyer, was unmarried, and seemingly unmoored to anything or anyone other than my two dogs.

"I am going to adopt a baby," I said into his rheumy eyes.

"Oh Lordy." Henry was not happy. He gaped at me like I had lost my mind.

"You can't give her back when you get tired," Ann said.

"I don't plan to," I assured her. "I'm ready to be a mother."

We were all very quiet. I had no intention of pulling the plug on motherhood and hoped my declaration would be accepted without an argument.

Mr. Practical had an important question. "Who is going to keep your baby while you're at work?"

Ann chimed in. "I can't babysit. I'm too old, but I will help you any way I can."

"Day care. I already took care of that."

Henry exhaled and left the kitchen.

Ann and Henry had already raised two generations of kids. I didn't expect them to weigh in again. Ann was eighty-two years old, fiercely trying to keep Alzheimer's disease from completely ravaging her sister and best friend, Ethel. She spent most of her days at Ethel's house or out front watering the grass. She and Henry were slowing down and weren't going to the movies as often. Eventually, she stopped attending her water aerobics class, so I knew leaning on them was not an option.

Sensing that I was sincere, Ann grudgingly conceded.

Since the cat was out of the bag, I called Helen, my cousin

Ray, and Kareem the next day. Ray and his wife, Rosalind, were ecstatic. "That is beautiful! Let us know how we can help."

Helen, who had no children, was less than enthused. "Why, Nef? Your life is perfect. Why would you ruin it like that? I thought we were going to be career gals together."

"I don't know where you got that from. I'm the last person to work a nine-to-five." I laughed. "I always wanted to be a mom."

"You never mentioned it to me."

"I don't talk about a lot of stuff, but that doesn't make my decision any less real."

In true snarky Helen form, she remarked, "I guess." She rushed off the phone, but I knew she wasn't finished finding the perfect negative thing to say.

I called Kareem. "I don't know if you've heard, but I am going to adopt a baby." I geared myself for whatever foolishness would come next.

"Oh my God, you are always doing something weird."

"Becoming a mother isn't weird," I said.

"You going to Korea?" He snorted.

"Nope. The County."

"Why would you adopt a crack baby?"

Inside, I bristled. You would think that he would be sympathetic to children whose parents couldn't take care of them. But Kareem's reaction wasn't unexpected. Not only did white people believe that nonsense the media spread about kids in the foster system, Black people did too.

"They're not all crack babies," I said. There was no point in trying to explain nurture versus nature to him, so I let it go.

"Well, the mama must be a prostitute. I mean, who else would get with a ho?"

"Goodbye, Kareem." I was disheartened that a member of my own family couldn't see beyond the racist propaganda that defined Black foster children.

A few days later, I even called my mother, though I'm sure Helen or my brother had already told her about my plan. Her once fly lifestyle had long since become a distant memory. She was working as a licensed vocational nurse in Houston for thirteen dollars an hour. "I don't know what to say," Diane said. "I mean, do you ever plan to have your own children?" She sounded alarmed.

"Any child I adopt will be my own," I said.

"You know what I mean." She sighed.

I did. As a young adult, I figured I would have biological children because that's what everyone around me did, and I felt like there were so many wrongs from my own childhood to be righted. Biological motherhood would give me that avenue to fix a few things. I would fiercely protect my child and never leave them. I pictured myself welcoming a son or daughter into the world and searching their face for my freckles and their dad's ears. I loved perusing sexy maternity clothing and wondered if pregnancy would be kind to my body. As I entered my thirties, however, the idea of creating a biological family lost its luster. I wanted to be a parent, and I didn't have to wait on marriage or pregnancy.

"Do you know the people?" Her question was indicative of how the Black community saw legal adoption.

"Nope."

"So, you're going to get a baby from a family you don't know." She was trying to make me feel like I had not thought this through.

I couldn't believe she was giving me grief about formally adopting a child when I had grown up the product of a Black adoption by her parents. "That's generally how it works."

"Boy? Girl? Do you get to choose?"

"I want a little Black boy, aged six months or less, at least half African American, without alcoholism, crystal meth, or schizophrenia in his direct lineage." I had already imagined my son, and when I completed the match paperwork, those were the boxes I checked.

"Okay, but what if something is wrong with him?"

"I'll cross that bridge when I come to it. The County has a lot of services for the kids." I was not offended by her concerns because I knew she was having a cultural reaction to how families were created in the Black community. Adopting a child I did not know was breaking code. White people did shit like that.

"Lots of Black people adopt, you know," I said.

"Yeah, but they're rich." She was thinking of celebrities who flew to foreign countries and paid thousands of dollars in adoption fees to bring home babies.

"You don't have to be rich to adopt." I could have given her the abbreviated version of how formal adoption worked to allay her fears, but she was my fourth call about this same subject, and I was over the condescension from her, Helen, and my brother.

Exasperated, Diane said, "I'm going to have to call you back."

She didn't say it out loud, but I knew what she was thinking. *Something must be wrong with those children.* She probably called Helen or Kareem next so they could laugh at how stupid I was for taking on someone else's reject, which was ironic given that our family tree was littered with informal Black adoptions. But it didn't matter. My family thought I was messing up my life.

Without question, Black adoption was embedded in my DNA and the unconscious foundation for my decision to formally adopt a non-family member. My family should have seen that one coming. Motherhood, however I achieved it, was my decision. Neither outcome—cultural rule breaker or outlier—was my plan. I just wanted a baby.

Graduating into Motherhood

"Hey, Nef, it's Donna. You got a minute?"

Donna's call snapped me out of my boredom. I had been sitting at my desk, plotting an escape from my current job writing press releases and articles about the gains the agency was making with its first female president at the helm. I needed something more flexible or at the very least, a work environment in more beautiful surroundings. Outside my window was a grassy area with several beautiful maple trees and just beyond, the contradiction of asphalt, rocks, and train tracks. The industrial building was east of the 110 Freeway and still blighted from the 1992 riots. I was also in charge of updating the company website. My role wasn't as exciting as I initially thought it would be, and I filled my ample free time working on my novel. But as I held the phone to my ear, my gripes seemed insignificant. Donna was about to fulfill my dream of motherhood. Immediately, I grabbed a pen and paper.

"Absolutely."

She told me about Micah, who was nine months old, biracial, and presented with a few developmental delays. He was unable to sit up on his own, wave, or smile. He would receive occupational therapy for the physical delays and would more than likely need assistance with cognitive and behavioral development. Those were large words with big responsibilities and huge ramifications if I got his treatment wrong. I asked to meet Micah and was told that unless I was committed to accepting the placement, the answer was no. I would have to agree to foster on the front end. DCFS had specific rules about prospective foster/adoptive parents meeting foster children. The biggest mistake prospective parents made was falling in love with a child without understanding the gravity of their special needs. Even practical, smart people watched their common sense fly out the window when presented with an adorable baby. Their focus on getting a child overshadowed the time and stiff learning curve associated with parenting a child with special needs. Donna continued sharing details about Micah, and in the back of my mind, I heard Ann saying, "You can't give him back when you get tired." I put down my pen.

"Can I call you back?" I stared at the slow-moving traffic from my office window and searched my heart. Micah would be my first child, my first foray into motherhood as a single parent. Could I support a child with special needs? Would he outgrow those challenges? Was my life set up to help him catch up on age-appropriate milestones like smiling and waving? I knew the answer. I called Donna back. "I can't do it. I'm sorry."

Donna was chipper and assured me that the most important thing was being able to determine what I could and could not handle. She said that people got in over their heads all the time, and it was better not to go down that road, and that another placement would come in time.

———————

I didn't get another call for three months. It was the beginning of June, and I was in the car fulfilling my role as chauffeur to Miss Daisy, a.k.a. Ann Hawthorne. Once or twice per month, I drove Ann to her sister Ethel's home in Carson, twenty-five minutes outside of Los Angeles, so Ann could take care of some household chores for Ethel, who was slipping further and further into dementia.

The early symptoms of Aunt Ethel's Alzheimer's disease came in the form of back-to-back phone calls to my grandparents. Aunt Ethel would forget she had just called and call so many times that they would take the phone off the hook. Eventually, her son Ray had to disconnect the stove so she would not burn herself or the food. Aunt Ethel, like Ann, was a world-class cook and losing that ability was devastating. As a result, Ann prepared meals for Ethel—greens, cornbread, chicken wings, or steak—and brought them on every visit. Ann and I had made this trip countless times. On this particular day, we were cruising down the highway when Donna called. "I have another placement."

I pulled the car onto the shoulder of the freeway as Ann

looked on. Another baby boy was available. Allen was three months old, born to a sixteen-year-old girl and a twenty-nine-year old man. The couple was supposed to bring the baby to DCFS later that day. Three months was a little young, I thought, but I agreed to foster the baby. Then Donna dropped two whammies. First, the teenager did not want to give up her baby permanently, but neither she nor the father were ready to parent. The County would mandate parenting classes and other services to prepare her for motherhood. With family support, she could get her baby back, but there was no timetable on when, or if, that would happen. I would agree to take the baby, knowing that there would be some back and forth until the girl, her family, or the baby's dad got themselves together. In other words, there was a slim chance of my keeping Allen forever. The second issue was that the mother was a flight risk. She had run away with her son's father before and might flee again. Donna said I did not have to decide right then and would call me when the girl and Allen arrived.

We hung up, and I merged back onto the freeway. Ann, who was excited, asked if I needed to go home to get ready. I explained that I was on hold until Donna called back. I already had diapers and clothing for the baby, and would not make any additional purchases before he arrived. We continued to Aunt Ethel's, where Ann changed her bed linen, fed her, and arranged the leftover food in the refrigerator.

My mind was in the clouds. It might really happen this time. I spoke briefly with Lori, who reiterated what Donna said about this being strictly a fostering situation. Lori said that a relative would probably come forward to take the baby and urged me not to get too attached. I tried to distract myself by cleaning Aunt Ethel's already-clean house.

A few hours later, after I returned home, Donna called again. Allen's social worker would bring him to me that evening. It was time to set things in motion. I called Nancy to let her know that I would be bringing a baby to her the following week. I checked to make sure I had enough diapers, washed the dishes, and started a load of laundry. I tossed out the newspaper and even dusted my bookcase. With at least two hours to kill, I took my dogs for a walk. We got halfway down the block when my cell phone buzzed again. It was Donna. Allen and his mom and dad were missing. They hadn't shown up to DCFS, and no one knew where they were. She would call me tomorrow.

Near tears, I called Nancy back. "Thanks for being on standby, but I won't need you after all." I couldn't believe how quickly I got emotionally invested on a maybe.

"What happened?" She sounded concerned.

After I explained the situation, she said, "That's not your baby. You're going to know when it is, and it won't be all this drama." I loved Nancy. She kept it real, and she was right. I called Donna and told her I wanted no part of the Bonnie-and-Clyde situation. There were too many red flags and other children who needed a home.

Two weeks later, my besties and I were scheduled to go to

Palm Springs. It was time for my annual birthday getaway, a tradition we had been enjoying for over a decade. I loved Palm Springs. The pace was slow, the food was great, and shopping at the outlets was stupendous. The plan was to lie by the pool in triple-digit weather, get massages, drink too much, and act wild on the dance floor. I had been looking forward to the getaway, but something in my spirit made me think that Donna would call about a new placement, and I canceled the trip. Sure enough, the day after my birthday, Donna had the perfect match. "Kemarye is six months old, strong, determined, handsome, legally free for adoption, and self-soothes himself to sleep. Are you interested?"

"Heck, yeah!" I was elated.

"Could you come to my office around lunchtime to receive more information?" Donna sounded hopeful.

"I can come now if you like." Something was different about that phone call. Call it superstition, but I thought the third time had to be the charm. Kemarye was everything I had asked for: a Black baby boy at the right age, with no fetal alcohol syndrome or crystal meth in his lineage. He just had to be the one.

"I have a short meeting in about ten minutes." Donna laughed at my unabashed eagerness. "Don't worry, he'll still be available at lunchtime."

"Sounds good."

I tried not to speed to her office in Torrance, not too far from where I had taken PS-MAPP training. I signed in and waited patiently in the lobby, watching mothers and social workers talk while kids bounced up and down on the hard plastic seats. The room had off-white linoleum tile and colorful brochures in English and Spanish announcing how to access WIC vouchers, First Five vaccinations, Head Start programs, child abuse hotlines, and regional center services. I kept my mind open. As happy as I was, I did not want to miss anything Donna had to share about Kemarye.

Donna emerged, all smiles. She had a brown file folder with a photo, papers detailing the baby's family history and previous foster care placements, and a blurry video of him playing with a white bunny rabbit. Kemarye was the seventh child of a woman whose six older children were also in out-of-home placement. Three had been adopted, and the eldest three boys were in the same foster home.

The baby's mother, Renata, really wanted Kemarye, even though she was a known addict. Knowing he would be detained in the hospital because he would probably test positive for drugs, she delivered Kemarye at home. A few hours after his birth, she took him to the hospital, where they both received medical attention. Renata tried to control his placement by sending an aunt and two neighbors to claim him, but neither could pass the background check required to take him home. Kemarye's father was incarcerated. With no other family in a position to take Kemarye, he went into foster care.

His first foster placement, with a woman named Ms. Henderson, lasted two months. Ms. Henderson had five other kids, and Kemarye screamed constantly. She had not made arrangements with her landlord to have foster children and was on the verge of being evicted. Kemarye was moved to the home of Mrs. Wilson, the mother of an adult son, a teenage boy, and six foster children. Her husband had died years before, and she was a professional foster mother. She was known to take great care of kids but had no desire to adopt. My head was swimming. This sounded too good to be true. I waited for a shoe to drop, a bomb to fall, a zinger to crash our meeting. I couldn't stop looking at Kemarye's photo. He had sweet cheeks and a small brown Afro. He was smiling and curious about the phone he was being recorded on and kept reaching for it.

"What a cutie," Donna cooed.

What a blessing, I thought. *The video does not do the little fellow justice.*

"Do you have time to meet him?"

"Right now?"

"Yes." She was serious.

"This is happening so fast." I was trying not to hyperventilate. "Let's go."

I followed Donna to Mrs. Wilson's home in Watts, all the while willing my heart to remain in my chest. I was giddy and overjoyed. My life was about to change, and I was pumped. Mrs. Wilson's beige house was replete with a white stone facade, neatly trimmed green grass, and an ornate brown wrought-iron gate that enclosed the front yard. It was the best-kept home on the block, and my son was inside.

Before I even crossed the threshold, Mrs. Wilson asked if I was a Christian. Donna had warned me that religion was important to Mrs. Wilson. "Yes," I quickly answered. I would not call myself the most devout Christian, but I did believe in a power greater than myself. Mrs. Wilson had no control over Kemarye's placement for adoption but exerted a faux ownership of this portion of the process, and I hoped I would pass her inspection.

From the moment I saw him, it was obvious Kemarye had been loved on. At the half-year mark, my future son was a strapping baby boy, curious and in midstride of a special ops crawl. My breath caught in my throat as Mrs. Wilson led us inside her immaculate house. After getting settled on a floral sofa covered in plastic, I was struck by how Jesus lived in this home. His presence was in the framed biblical platitudes and numerous crosses that decorated the walls. I lied effortlessly when Mrs. Wilson asked which church I belonged to and politely said *yes* to all of her other questions. Honestly, I don't remember the details of the conversation. The only sound I really heard was my heart beating furiously in my chest. Kemarye was the one.

I watched him pull himself up on the couch where I was sitting. His striped blue, yellow, and white polo and blue shorts were so cute, and his big brown eyes were clear with purpose. I hesitated to scoop him into my arms. I was a stranger, but I felt as if I already knew him. Sensing I wanted to hold him, Mrs. Wilson encouraged me to pick him up.

Kemarye was exceeding developmental milestones in his

ability to sit up and roll over, his grabbing action, and his attempts at crawling. His little curly Afro was soft, and he had a love affair with his right index and middle fingers. I patted his back and sat him on my lap, and he gripped my thumb. Donna asked if I was in love as she snapped pictures of us. "Yes," I answered, though my real feeling was deeper than love. It was a knowing. Kemarye was my son.

In the photo, which Donna gave me later, my eyes are focused on the miracle sitting on me and his yellow-and-white ducky bib, damp with baby slobber. A smile emanates from my soul and lights up my entire face. Kemarye's expression is serious.

He did not know what was going on, but a divide clearly formed on that day: There was my life *before* laying eyes on this beautiful child, and my life *after*, and I knew in that moment that I would never be the same. I imagined Kemarye and I tooling around town in my MINI Cooper with the sunroof open, enjoying the sunshine, hanging out at the library, riding the train at Travel Town. Even after five minutes, I knew there was nothing I wouldn't do for him.

I wanted to take Kemarye home immediately, but the County didn't move that fast. As a consolation, I was allowed to visit him the following week. Kemarye and I would be courting. Lori once told me that chemistry was the key to determining whether or not a match would work with a baby. Infants did not have words and there would be no *I like taking walks in the park, what about you?* She wasn't talking about passion, but a visceral attraction. If I didn't feel a connection with him, we could still be together but our bond would not be as strong.

I reflected on my relationship with my mother and with the guys I had dated. We may have had physical chemistry but nothing that tied us together emotionally or spiritually. But Kemarye and I had it all. It was an unspoken, mutual connection reserved for soul mates.

On the drive back to work that afternoon, the joy I felt was so overwhelming that I had to pull to the curb. I had been so cool in front of Mrs. Wilson and Donna, answering questions like it was an everyday thing to meet my future son. Inside, the butterflies in my stomach threatened to take me away. I called my colleague, Tyrone. A married father and grandfather, he was very supportive of my plan to adopt and the only person in the office who knew that I was searching for a child. I attempted to tell him everything, but my words were jumbled. Tyrone instructed me to breathe. "Of course, you're excited and nervous," he said patiently. "You'll be fine." I wish I could have articulated how I felt, but the words were not available. The best description of the moment was wonder. Kemarye was the manifestation of a journey begun ten months earlier. He was a wish fulfilled and a dream come true.

On Thursday, August 2, I was fidgety. I'd sit up and then lie down on my black velvet couch with bold flowers printed on the seat back and arms. *Grey's Anatomy* played on the TV as I kept an anxious eye on the front door. I double then triple-checked my baby care supplies, walked LL and Sunday for the fifth time, and fielded phone calls from excited friends. Cathy, a social worker from DCFS, would be bringing Kemarye home, and everyone wanted to know: *Is he there yet? When can I come by?*

I was expecting them in the evening around five, then seven o'clock. Finally, at 9:40 p.m., Cathy arrived. She held Kemarye in one arm and a carpet bag overflowing with clothes in the other. She handed him to me and removed the foster care placement paperwork from her briefcase. I snuggled my baby boy and blindly signed on the dotted line. Those papers could have said anything. I didn't care. I would move heaven and earth to give Kemarye the best life possible. Cathy gave me information about post-adoption services and said she would return the following week to check on him. Twenty minutes later, we were alone. Mother and son.

———————

Kemarye was surprisingly heavy. He did not struggle to get down, though his bright eyes were as big as saucers. He sucked on his fingers as I took him on a tour of my—now *our*—small one-bedroom apartment. I formally introduced him to his canine brother and sister. He regarded the dogs with interest. We sat on the couch, and I removed his powder-blue socks so the dogs could lick his feet and hands. Kemarye tried to pet them, and they tried to jump on him to get to his sweet slobbery face. Grateful that he was unafraid of animals and did not sneeze or cough, I relaxed.

Kemarye turned his intent gaze on me. "Oh, you want to know my name? It's Mommy." I kissed his little face. "I'm your mama and I love you." And I loved calling myself *Mommy*.

We were both keyed up and exhausted, and it was bedtime. I changed his diaper, gave him a bottle of formula, and put him in his pajamas. We went into our bedroom and headed to his crib. I set him down, and he screamed. I picked him up, and he was quiet. I tried putting him down again, and he wailed. I was confused. Hadn't Donna said that he self-soothed? During both visits, Mrs. Wilson reiterated that Kemarye slept through the night. What was happening? I knew how to put kids to bed, but this was my first child, and he would not stop crying. Could the neighbors hear him? What were they thinking? I hoped no one called the child abuse hotline. Near midnight, I couldn't take it anymore and called Lori. "I'm failing at parenting, and it's my first day."

She talked me down. "He does not know you, and he's off schedule." She yawned. "Try rocking him."

I took her advice, and at some point, we both passed out.

His Name Is *What?*

From the moment I knew I was ready to become a mother,
I had been thinking of baby names. Would I go on trend and
choose Caden, Jayden, Jordan, Logan, or Chance? Go classic
with Michael, Christopher, David, or Marcus? Dig in the family
archives for Henry or John? I could try an old-school name like
Samuel, Clyde, or Lawrence, or make a racially conscious choice
like my parents did and mine the motherland for Sundiata Akita
or Lumumba. Knowing I wanted a child who was at least half-
Black, I might honor our community and reach for André, Taurus,
Semaj, Booker, Tre-breh, or Antoine. There was no shortage of
creative names among Black people, who subconsciously remembered a time when they could not take ownership of naming their
babies. The internet had hundreds of baby-boy-name listicles. I
kept telling myself that my son would come with a name, and I
knew that a new name would reshape his identity and define my
role as his mother.

During the PS-MAPP training, prospective foster/adoptive parents were taught to accept a child in all his glory. Names, like religious practices, were links to their heritage. We were to respect and uphold those traditions. To ignore or deny such cultural markers suggested the child's origins were insignificant. Abrupt changes had the ability to destroy a child's self-esteem, causing him to feel lost and isolated. It was the foster/adoptive parent's responsibility to do everything in her power to ease his transition from ward of the state to forever family. I was totally on board with these recommendations, even though I already had a name in mind. I was a huge fan of playwright August Wilson and loved that August meant *grand* and *inspiring reverence or admiration*. I knew I wasn't the first foster/adoptive parent to consider changing a child's name and suspected it was a common occurrence, especially with infants. But what about toddlers? Was it even ethical to change the name of a three- or four-year-old person? Would the new name cause additional confusion for a child who had an attachment with his biological or foster parents and was moved from their home to a new placement with a strange lady who declared, *I'm your mama*? Mix in a new school, siblings, friends, and the navigation of a new neighborhood. All of the sudden newness, with its good intentions, was a guaranteed recipe for shutting down or acting out.

I met a fellow adoptive mom who also changed her foster son's name. Eighteen years earlier, Cynthia's son was two years old when they became a forever family. Not a fan of the birth parents' selected name, she dropped the first syllable and called him by the last half of his given name. Before he knew it, she capitalized the final syllable then added the middle name of the men in her family. *Voilà!* A new designation. I got it. The plans we had for our boys were light years north, south, east, and west of where they were born. Kemarye would not know the difference until he was older.

In 2003, an old debate was resurrected with a CBS News article, "Black Names a Résumé Burden?" A century ago, whites and Blacks more or less shared race-neutral names like Donna, Linda, Sandra, Robert, and Adam. In the 1960s, Stokely Carmichael stirred souls with Black Power and a hypercultural awareness of ties to Africa and intimated that the Anglo-Saxon names of the 1940s and 1950s were outdated and corny. My parents were certainly of this mindset, as they shed their slave names and gave me and Kareem African and Arabic names. While those African connections were necessary and relevant in the late 1960s through the 1970s, I agreed with the CBS News article that some folks got too imaginative and now their adult children's resumes were placed in the round file. Even so, I understood this creativity to be an act of resistance. We should be free to name our children whatever we want, without stigma. The article further cited a study that concluded after responding to 1,300 classified ads with dummy resumes, the authors found Black-sounding names were 50 percent less likely to get a callback than white-sounding names with comparable resumes.

Kemarye's government name was Kemarye Lester Jefferson,

which was fine for the block but too musical for the hills. Translation: My baby needed a new name. Naming in the Black community was political, sacred, and sometimes made people ask, *His name is what?* Names denoted geography, political thrust of an era, social and economic status. They situated us in our tribe, advertised our ambitions, and sometimes defined our life path. Naming was powerful and explained why people spent months thinking of just the right name for their baby.

Anyone who saw *Roots* knew that Kunta Kinte was adamant that he not be called Toby. At the time of his capture, he was old enough to know his native tongue, his parents, and the long history of his tribe, the Mandinkas of Juffure. Once on American shores and the property of another man, Kunta was forced by lash to concede to the name Toby. At night, when the overseer was out of sight, Kunta secretly prayed to Allah and recited the names of his ancestors. He was proud of his heritage and never lost connection to the land that birthed him—a powerful acknowledgment of the significance of naming in our culture.

There were alternate perspectives on the ramifications of Black-sounding names. In an academic article, "The Causes and Consequences of Distinctively Black Names," the authors posited: "Among Blacks born in the last two decades, names provide[d] a strong signal of socio-economic status, which was not previously the case. We find, however, no negative causal impact of having a distinctively Black name on life outcomes. Although that result is seemingly in conflict with previous audit studies involving resumes, we argue that the two sets of findings can be reconciled." The data would be reconciled when Black folks were the resume gatekeepers. We needed to be the ones to vet Lozenge-Nay Jackson's paperwork and, if everything was in order, place it in the tray marked *to be interviewed*.

I made this point at my monthly book club meeting. We were talking about Edward P. Jones's *The Known World*, drinking pinot noir, eating shrimp étouffée, and discussing this very topic. We were all college-educated, Black professionals, and three out of five of us had kids. We agreed that Black people needed to be globally competitive, especially on the corporate level. Made-up names, like too many tattoos or piercings on Black skin, would amount to extra strikes in an already uneven playing field, thus, limiting opportunities for Blacks to get ahead economically and socially. More live and let live than my compatriots, I accused them of being snobs, though I was equally amused by some of the names. My friend Alita had a friend Naomi, who named her daughter Solomon. Alita assumed Naomi gave her daughter a boy's name to ensure a callback on future resumes. Naomi challenged her by listing the names of their friends—Fadonna, China, Keeta, Kenya, Malika. She reminded Alita that they were all very successful with medical and law degrees, six-figure incomes, and tenured college professorships. Because of their success, Naomi wasn't worried about a résumé. She liked the name Solomon and didn't have to bend gender-naming rules to ensure that her daughter would taste success as an adult.

White people in America had the power, so they made rules regarding which baby names were economically acceptable. So, Apple Peterson's resume would be pushed up the food chain because both white and Black gatekeepers would assume that Apple was white. While the Black community's naming process was similar to that of whites (family trees, classic literature, spiritual and religious influences, and socioeconomic status directly impacted naming choices), white privilege shielded white people from worrying their child's first name would interfere with or deny them employment opportunities. Aristocratic names like Fitzgerald conjured images of old money, wealth, and power, not a little Black boy, unless he was upper-middle class or poor and his mama had high aspirations. Whatever the reason, the mighty job application was the line in the sand.

I did not change Kemarye's name to fit a particular image, but rather to give him a new start. I chose a name that bespoke the arts, global travel, higher education, service to others, and success. My baby didn't know it but my Black Power lineage, middle-class upbringing, and bourgeoisie Bohemian lifestyle had informed my decision to choose a name that would reflect his new familial lineage. I informed Cathy that Kemarye Lester Jefferson would now be known as August. Changing his name made him mine. Satisfied with my son's new name, I gave my friends the green light to stop by to meet August for the first time. Lori and her son came over bright and early the day after August's placement. They were our first visitors.

"You survived your first night as a mom." Lori smiled knowingly.

"Barely." I chuckled.

She handed me a blue envelope with *August* written across it. Inside was a Target gift card for four hundred dollars. She and my other friends had pooled their funds and surprised us. I was humbled by the unexpected, generous gift and practically ran to the bathroom. I didn't want them to see me cry. Lori said, "Trust me, you're going to need every nickel." They stayed for a little while, and I basked in the glow of August's presence. Seeing his name in print made the moment real.

Ann and Henry came over later that evening. They were dressed like they were going out to dinner. August was asleep, and Ann tiptoed into our room, Henry close on her heels. "What's his name again?" Henry said.

"August," I said with pride.

"That's a strong name." Henry gave me the okay signal. "What a big boy!"

"Shh." Ann shot Henry a don't-wake-the-baby look.

"No worries. He's out for the night."

"So precious," Ann cooed, stroking his Afro. After all of their worries about me adopting by myself, they were relaxed and happy for me. They patiently waited an hour, hoping August would wake up, but he slept right on through the night.

On Saturday, my apartment was overrun with August's new cousins, aunties, and uncles. Everyone wanted to know when the adoption would be final. I told them I wasn't sure, and I expected the process to take at least a year, maybe longer. Once the stampede of well-wishers left and we were alone, I happily collapsed on the couch. Introducing August to his new world made us a family. I was born again and in service to a power greater than myself: love.

Motherhood So White

I had my son's name settled but still couldn't get much rest. Already a light sleeper, I leapt out of bed and over to his crib every time he rolled over, making sure he was breathing. I was high on adrenaline and using muscle memory to make bottles, change diapers, and forage through his drawer for a bib to match his many onesies. This was our new normal. Suddenly I was the mother of a Black child, and I needed to educate myself on my new role.

With my sweet boy in tow, we went to the library. "Excuse me, are there any books in this building by or for Black mothers?"

The research librarian pursed his lips. "That's a good question." He clicked and clicked computer keys and wrote down two names, Yvonne Bynoe and Rebecca Walker.

"Anything else?"

"No, I'm sorry." His cheeks reddened with embarrassment.

Of course, I already knew the answer. My journey to

motherhood as a Black woman was not part of mainstream culture's idea of motherhood, and thus, there would be no funny or ballsy mommy books written by Black mothers on the shelf. Our absence from literature and prime-time media prevented us, as Kimberly Seals Allers described in her *New York Times* article, "Hollywood to Black Mothers: Stay Home," from being "seen as thinkers in this mommy movement, women with an important perspective in shaping the future of, say, maternity leave and child-care issues." If we could get past our two Americas with white mothers in one corner and Black mothers in the other, mainstream culture would see more similarities than differences. Everyone knew at least one woman who experienced an *oops* pregnancy or struggled with whether God intended for her to have children naturally. This ongoing polarization of Black motherhood and white motherhood exacerbated a trust problem that made becoming allies with white feminists, whose interests remained gender-centered and short on racial issues, difficult. As long as the default definition of mother in America meant *white woman*, not only would the status quo remain, but white mothers of Black boys would have no point of reference when their sons found themselves on the wrong side of a police baton.

"No worries, I'm used to it." I wheeled August over to the kids' section to play with puppets and trains.

Figuring Beverly Hills was the wrong neighborhood to find what I was looking for, I went to the Black bookstore, then to the internet, and finally braved a big box bookstore looking for books on how to handle marginalization. I came away empty-handed. Motherhood was cliquish, with tried-and-true recipes for white people but nothing for single, adoptive Black mothers. Early on, I had assumed it would be easy to find culturally relevant information about Black people who adopted. I wanted to know what happened when a Black woman went outside her community to adopt a child she did not know. I needed specific advice on how to handle the social and emotional consequences of becoming a single mother in a country where the term *single mother* was code for *Black welfare mother*. This trope was used from presidential candidate Governor Ronald Reagan to President Clinton and later to President Trump, who approved campaign ads asserting that Black, single mothers were siphoning millions of dollars from tax-paying (read: white) citizens.

So, I turned to the media, hoping to catch a glimpse of myself. Movies like *Knocked Up*, *Baby Mama*, and *Stepmom*, among others, all featured white women. These mainstream images of white, single motherhood celebrated *oops* pregnancies, surrogates, sperm banks, and stepmoms, and empowered white women to choose their own path to parenthood. I didn't bother going to see these films. I did not need another reminder of what white motherhood looked like.

Six months into the parenting gig, I was getting used to operating with little to no sleep, but I was still on the hunt for something that came close to reflecting my story. Curating information was my superpower. I should have had no trouble tapping the well of parenting resources that existed in the universe. Boy, was I surprised to learn that my quest for narratives about Black mothers would be like looking for a needle in a haystack, but the white woman's story would be told over and over, paving the way for her christening as *badass* for becoming a single mother by choice.

What about my *badass* choice for pursuing adoption on my own? Didn't that warrant a book or romantic comedy, or at the very least an interesting, diverse perspective on motherhood? While Black adoption was common in my community, I was an outlier for wanting to adopt a child I did not know. I was also an outlier among whites for defying stereotypes around single, Black motherhood, but none of this was in writing. When you can't find an experience reflected in art or literature or film, it's hard to believe that it even exists. And yet, I was real and so was August.

A search for single mothers on the small screen led me to 1992 when Murphy Brown, a fictional white woman, earned feminist accolades for going against the status quo. During season four of the sitcom *Murphy Brown*, young women my age witnessed the final change in social mores regarding unwed pregnant women. Women were encouraged to spend less time trying to get men to make honest women out of them and more time on personal fulfillment. Women were advised to expect more from intimate relationships, which was in direct opposition to what their mothers had accepted. This conscious uncoupling of marriage being the only path to fulfillment delayed marriage and childbirth for decades, giving women time to catch up with men economically, socially, and politically. As a divorced, investigative reporter at the top of her game, Murphy Brown epitomized those gains and continued to push the envelope of motherhood after learning she was pregnant. The character didn't have a moral dilemma regarding her *oops* pregnancy, as her choice boiled down to whether she would coparent or be a single mother. Murphy opted for single motherhood, reinforcing the idea that motherhood was not synonymous with marriage or two parents.

This fictional character's decision to go it alone prompted major backlash from the 1992 vice presidential candidate Senator Dan Quayle. In a family-values speech, Quayle famously turned a personal issue into a political one when he said, "Prime time TV has Murphy Brown, a character who supposedly epitomizes today's intelligent, highly paid professional woman, mocking the importance of fathers by bearing a child alone and calling it another lifestyle choice." Quayle's comment polarized America and positioned single mothers as the antithesis of conservative moral values. Meanwhile, feminists embraced Murphy Brown as a hero. According to Sara McLanahan's "The Consequences of Single Motherhood," she was symbolic of "the moral right of women to pursue careers and raise children on their own." Murphy's choice reflected the lives of many working single mothers, who deserved to be included in the parenting paradigm as one type of family configuration. However, while I celebrated the strides of the single mother, I was quick to note that Murphy Brown, the purveyor of modern, single motherhood, was, unsurprisingly, white. Her triumphant stance for lifestyle choices did not shape my idea of motherhood.

I continued to wonder who would tell my story. My grandmothers and Black television mom Clair Huxtable from *The Cosby Show* had already stamped an indelible picture of what it was supposed to mean to be a mother for me. I heard *Julia* was groundbreaking with its widowed, single, Black professional mother, but 1968 was before my time and there had been no reruns of the show during my formative years. When I was a young adult in the 1990s, Black television loosened up a little and offered diversity among Black family situation comedies. *The Parkers* featured a single Black mother and *Sister, Sister* showed a professional adoptive mother. Both single Black mothers were looking for a man, not making a political statement about being a single mother by choice. These images were close but did not fully match the mother I wanted to become.

The closest Black women came to celebrating single motherhood in the media was Cheryl Pepsii Riley's 1988 powerful anthem "Thanks for My Child." Riley sang about a woman suddenly left to parent a baby alone. The song was not just for single Black mothers, nor was it a glorification of motherhood outside of wedlock. Rather, it was a message of strength for all single mothers to remember that their baby, however he came, was a blessing. The song was a huge hit on Black radio and even peaked at number thirty-two on *Billboard magazine's* "Hot 100" list, and should have led to the dismantling of the myth of the Black welfare mother.

If white feminists were aware of Riley's song, it could have been a bridge to unite mothers against our white-male-dominated society. But because Black mothers' struggles were invisible or negatively stereotyped, white feminists missed an opportunity to see how racism and discrimination in employment and housing forced situations where poor women of color became single mothers, not as a lifestyle choice but out of necessity. Black women's marriages and partnerships were disrupted by incarceration, premature death, and drug abuse leaving these communities run by mothers and grandmothers. This was in stark contrast to the "universalized experience of white middle-class women who had the option of staying home to raise their children," described by Bonnie Thornton Dill in "Feminism, Race, and the Politics of Family Values." These separate-but-unequal designations in motherhood continued in the media and the real world.

White women controlled who could get away with *oops* pregnancies. This was evident when Bristol Palin, daughter of 2008 Republican vice presidential nominee Governor Sarah Palin, became a mother at eighteen. The conservatives spun a tale of teenage mistakes and gave the young mother a pass. Black folks cried foul, knowing that if Sasha or Malia came up pregnant, the Obamas would have been shamed off the campaign trail. However, white society wasn't the only source of judgment. Black people were also guilty of judging single mothers at the grocery store, gas station, post office, and parent-teacher conferences, assuming they were irresponsible Black welfare mothers, rather than a woman in love or the maker of an innocent mistake. Single Black mothers were marginalized on both sides, and motherhood, one of the universal female experiences, found itself caught between two worlds, one Black, one white. Black people had our own set of religious and class beliefs, and strong feelings about bringing another nappy-headed baby with no daddy into the world. We had drunk the Kool-Aid poured by white people and believed an *oops* pregnancy brought the race's curve down. Would that be the assumption from whites and Blacks when my son and I strolled down the street or played at the park? In the twenty-first century, would Black family life persist as diametric opposites: *Good Times* or *The Cosby Show*, whose legacy was eventually characterized by lies and abuse?

The Murphy Brown effect reverberated in publishing, with scores of books penned almost exclusively by white women. Jane Mattes's *Single Mothers by Choice: A Guidebook for Single Women Who Are Considering or Have Chosen Motherhood*; *Adopting on Your Own: The Complete Guide to Adoption for Single Parents* by Lee Varon; *Choosing Single Motherhood: The Thinking Woman's Guide* by Mikki Morrissette; *Knock Yourself Up: No Man? No Problem: A Tell-All Guide to Becoming a Single Mom* by Louise Sloan; and other narratives stocked the parenting aisles with useful information, but still there wasn't any space devoted to mothers of color. We shared similar concerns about exes, financing single motherhood, and feeling emotionally overwhelmed. Race, economics, and culture ratcheted up how and why we chose solo parenting, and that information was nonexistent because our experiences did not exist beyond the bounds of our community. Despite the long history of relationships between Black mammies, nannies, housekeepers, and caregivers for white children, our consistent erasure in parenting literature confirmed that *mother* in America would always be read as white.

Black mother writers responded to this deficit with *Who's Your Mama? The Unsung Voices of Women and Mothers*. Edited by Yvonne Bynoe, this compilation was described as follows in its description on Goodreads: "Unlike other motherhood books that focus on the experiences of a small group of affluent, married white women, *Who's Your Mama?* centers on the largely untold perspectives of the majority of diverse American women, whose unique and sometimes unconventional family structures impact our country." That was exactly what I was looking for. I was also grateful to read *Baby Love: Choosing Motherhood After a Lifetime of Ambivalence* by bestselling author and third-wave feminist, Rebecca Walker. Her memoir illustrated how a neglectful upbringing and tempestuous relationship with her Pulitzer Prize-winning mother, Alice Walker, complicated her own desire to become a mother. Boy, could I relate! Walker's disclosure of her privilege, bisexuality, fluency in liberal white feminist circles, and ultimate pregnancy demonstrated a unique approach to motherhood written by a Black woman.

Was that the extent of resources available? In 2008, when I was a new mother, it seemed so. I checked out Christian parenting circles, only to run into the same issue: motherhood seen only through a white lens. Those books tied women's identity to motherhood with faith-based principles for child-rearing. Other mom books professionalized motherhood to encourage stay-at-home moms to run their homes like businesses. While these options were meaningful for their intended audiences, there was nothing specific to Black mothers, forcing us to extrapolate the advice we needed to fit our cultural needs.

As of this writing in 2018, there were less than two dozen available books in print written by or for Black parents. Of this diminutive group, books by *New York Times* bestselling authors Denene Millner, adoptee Caroline Clarke, and Ylonda Gault Caviness resonated with me. Millner's book, *My Brown Baby: On the Joys and Challenges of Raising African American Children*, was a collection of parenting essays written by Black parents; Clarke's memoir described her search for her birth mother; and Caviness's book explored the lessons she learned from her mother about parenting and marriage. Each book offered an unabashedly Black perspective on motherhood, and oh, how I wished they were available ten years ago. I could have also benefitted from *Podcasts in Color*, featuring every type of Black mama ever invented, and Black parenting blog Mater Mea, among others, but they hadn't come online yet.

Back in the day, I was limited to joining Mocha Moms, other Black parenting organizations, or attending religious seminars. While I had subscriptions to a couple of Black parenting blogs, neither those outlets nor a church meeting was going to solve the core problem: *Mother* in America, ten years ago and now, equals white.

In Limbo

August had a new home, a new name, and a new family. In the eyes of the law, however, he was still a foster child, I was a foster mother, and our status would remain unchanged for two years. I gained a new respect for anyone willing to deal with birth parents, social workers, and DCFS. Fostering/adopting was an inexact science that demanded patience, flexibility, and organization from all participants. The guidelines were clear: birth parent visits, when possible; six months or more of social worker visits before parental rights were terminated; then weekly visits from the child's lawyer and social worker until the foster parent signed the adoption placement papers. After that, another wait of four to six months would pass before an adoption was finalized. Continuing education was optional and offered gratis to foster parents throughout the city. Many foster mothers held special certifications for children who had asthma, autism, and any other ailments that required medicine or breathing treatments. They spent time ferrying kids to specialists, dealt with teachers, and cared for a verboten demographic. Foster mothers flew under the radar unless a tragedy occurred. Far from the Black welfare queen, these primarily single women took on a responsibility that most coupled Blacks or whites with means and education would never embark upon. I was now one of these single Black women caring for a nonrelative, but I had no plans to ever foster again. I had my son.

My heart didn't know or care that eighteen months would pass before I signed adoption placement forms. August and I would behave as mother and son, and August's social worker, Cathy, would check on us every week. Her job was to assess August's emotional, physical, and psychological progress while in my care and to see if we were bonding. After the stampede of folks hugging, kissing, and posing in photos with him as my family brought him into our fold, August was very clear on who his mother was. He was not a clingy child, but would look in my direction whenever a new cheek was smashed against his. August was friendly, had sufficient toys, books, and Baby Einstein videos that he loved. August was in love with his day-care provider, Nancy, and his other favorite woman, Grandma Ann. He laughed easily, wiggled the corner bumpers loose from the furniture, pulled up on everything, and tried to eat the dogs' food. We had jam sessions with him on spoons and pot tops and me on dishes. I shared all of this with Cathy, who never stayed long. She approved of how well we were getting along, and this made the in-home visits tolerable rather than intrusive.

The weekly monitored visits with August's biological mother, Renata, were a different story. Though her parental rights had been terminated before August was placed with me, I was legally obligated to let Renata see him. Cathy monitored these visits at McDonald's or one of the DCFS offices. The schedule depended upon Renata's availability. I was usually given a four-hour window with hourly updates. Sometimes Renata did not show, and Cathy didn't want me to leave work for nothing.

On the days Renata confirmed her arrival, I'd leave work early, drive to Nancy's, pick up August, and drive to the designated meeting location. Driving him to see Renata could take up to an hour. Cathy, serving as liaison, would meet me in the parking lot. She'd hold August and his overstuffed diaper bag, with a small lovey, books, jar of bananas, spoon, and a prepared bottle. Feeding a child was as maternal as it was intimate. Theoretically, this small activity would assist Renata and August's bonding during the one-hour visit. I'd wait in the car, bugged about this interloper. The official timeline aside, I was already his mother. The County would never reunite August with Renata on a permanent basis because of her drug addiction, but they did insist that they spend time together. Because Renata was known to be emotional, Cathy thought it best that she and I not meet. I certainly wasn't up for a scene and resented supporting August's biological connection, but had agreed to this aspect of being a foster parent.

Initially, August did not seem affected by the visits, but by the third one, he became whiny and irritable. He'd spend the next couple of hours attached to me like Velcro. I hated to put him through this, but the law was the law. At their final visit, Cathy told me that August spit up all over Renata, who cried and handed him back.

"Really? She had a meltdown over baby vomit?" Only forty minutes had passed, and I was dozing in the parking lot when Cathy knocked on the window.

Cathy shrugged.

"How dare she be upset?" I was on fire. "He is an innocent baby and did what babies do."

"That's probably it for the visits."

"Over this?" *What a punk*, I thought.

"I've seen it before," Cathy said, heading to her car.

"I can't wait for this to be over."

Renata disappeared, and August never saw her again.

On paper, August's case was a slam dunk. The rights of both parents had been terminated, and I declared my intention to adopt him. But August had three older brothers still in the system and three siblings who had already been adopted. It was difficult keeping the ones in foster care together, and Renata added insult to injury by acting right just long enough to throw a wrench in any plans for permanency for them. The case was large and unwieldy, but August's placement was secure. I was in no danger of losing him. Overwhelmed with too many cases, Cathy transferred the case to a different social worker, and that worker bailed on us too, which delayed the entire process and directly impacted when August and I could become a forever family.

Somewhere along the way, we discovered that August did not have a birth certificate. Renata claimed she had it and strung the social worker along for four months with promises to get it to her. Two other social workers attempted to get it from the county recorder. Because his case was repeatedly transferred to new social workers, I was in charge of bringing each new person up to speed. With all of the turnover, I knew it would be easier for me to track down his birth certificate, and I did. Birth records for foster children were kept in Sacramento. I got the number and called repeatedly. Eventually, I connected with a sweet woman who took pity on me. She located August's birth certificate and sent it to me directly. Once I received it, there was still more waiting to do. None of this was covered in PS-MAPP training and, yet, foster parents were expected to keep accurate records and copies of everything. I was caring for just one child and couldn't imagine managing so many details for multiple children, as many foster parents did.

As we waited for the next steps in the adoption process, I continued settling into motherhood. I had all the hallmarks of a new mother and made a lot of rookie mistakes. It was much harder than I could have ever imagined. Since I had skipped pregnancy and didn't have baby weight to lose, I told myself I would avoid new mom traps like frumpiness or looking like a mom. I would not lose myself in the busyness of mothering. In my delusion, I was sure I'd rock my heels and wear skinny jeans and cute blouses. I would have the latest baby bag with hidden compartments, Velcro, and a pattern that screamed *cool mom*, and sport August on my chest or back in a Baby Bjorn.

Unsurprisingly, reality didn't quite live up to my expectations, especially when it came to finding a comfortable way to carry August. I tried every iteration: front carrier, shoulder seat, hip hugger, sling. I even channeled African and Asian moms who wrapped their babies in colorful cloth and placed them on their backs. Nothing worked. Unless I was holding August in my arms, he was too heavy in every position for my five-foot, 120-pound frame. I easily made seven trips to Target and Babies "R" Us making returns of various baby-wearing apparatuses. The verdict was clear: I would have to carry August in my arms until he could walk.

Fatigue was my next teacher. I crashed early in the evenings, right after August went down. Many nights I awoke on the couch, remote in hand, *Forensic Files* on the screen. I'd had no clue how utterly exhausting motherhood was and suddenly understood why couples fought over seemingly insignificant tasks. Even with my supportive family and friends, I had no daily backup in the house and all of August's needs fell on me. I never complained, which was another new mom error. I didn't feel like I deserved the luxury of complaining. I had chosen single motherhood and falsely believed that showing weakness meant my journey to motherhood through adoption was a mistake. No matter what, it was my decision, and I had to own all that came with it. I wanted to be everything to August to prove the haters wrong, especially one relative who sent my mother into a frenzy by telling her the County wasn't going to let me keep my son.

We were late to August's first pediatric appointment, which took place three weeks after he started living with me. I was every inch the new mother and underestimated how long it would take to get out of the car and up the elevator to the fourth floor. There was no way I could carry August, a diaper bag, jacket, an ill-fitting army-green baby carrier, and a folder containing his medical history. I had to reshuffle everything twice and finally settled on leaving the empty carrier snapped around my waist and carrying August. Out of breath, we spilled into the office overlooking Sunset Boulevard in West Hollywood looking like runaways. The nurse looked at my disheveled mess and smiled. "You must be Ms. Austin. Who do we have here?"

I started rambling. "I am adopting August, and he was placed with me three weeks ago. He has six siblings, Dr. Washington referred me. By the way, he said hi." I continued oversharing with Dr. Dolan, who listened intently as she examined August. He came in at 18.6 pounds and 29 inches at eight months. No wonder my back hurt. I went from carrying nothing bigger than an eight-pound Yorkie to carrying a full-fledged human being in the ninetieth percentile for height and weight overnight. My body was in shock. Dr. Dolan congratulated me and showed me August's growth chart. We discussed his vaccination schedule, and she told me to switch his formula to a soy-based brand to stem the spit up that inevitably stained the baby's bib and my tops. I was wearing one of those shirts with vomit on it, but hadn't even noticed when we left home.

Because I lived in Beverly Hills, I did not qualify for child-care assistance, so I supplemented the small monthly stipend I received from the County to pay Nancy. I used coupons from Women, Infants, and Children (WIC) for milk to purchase soy formula and then whole dairy milk after August turned one. The WIC store near my apartment was filled with Orthodox Jews who lived in the neighborhood. I chuckled every time I entered, wondering how President Reagan would spin this narrative about white people shopping at an establishment ostensibly created for "Black welfare queens." Parents were not allowed to split WIC coupons, and I would be stuck with four boxes of cereal, three bags of beans, two large jars of peanut butter, too many eggs, and multiple jugs of juice, which we did not drink. In an effort not to waste the food, I gave the extra items to Nancy and the neighbors. I wondered which genius at the state or federal level thought a toddler needed multiple boxes of cereal per month but no fresh fruit, fresh vegetables, diapers, or wipes. If the WIC program and the County were sincere about supporting the dietary needs of children, they needed to ask a real family what they ate.

There were many days I felt overwhelmed, and my body acted like it had actually been through the traumatic process of birth. A month later, I had a mild panic attack in the middle of the night. I was delirious from exhaustion and on my hands and knees, vomiting into the toilet. I kept repeating, "I know I did the right thing." The gravity of being a foster parent and all that it entailed finally sank in. I was somebody's mother and it felt good, but I was doing it alone and it was hard.

Looking for Diverse Parenting Literature in All the Right Places (and Finding Almost None)

Along with everything else that was going on, there was still mothering to be done. August needed to know that he was adopted. I began the adoption conversation with him early. There was no point in waiting or lying about his origins. There was no evidence of my carrying him in my womb and the earlier the word *adoption* was part of his lexicon, the better. In time, he would need language to explain to his friends where he came from. Books for transracial adoptions were everywhere with their glossy depictions of children of all races, creeds, and religions coming together under one roof with their white parents, but adoption books that featured Black children were difficult to find. Filled with beautiful, smiling photographs or lush illustrations, the emphasis in the transracial adoption books was humanity's similarities and love's ability to conquer all. Books about international adoptions reminded adoptive parents to honor Chinese, Ethiopian, Korean, Estonian, or Ecuadoran cultures. I found bilingual books and one that explained how a child from Malawi made her way to Topeka, Kansas, but nothing that mirrored August's experience of being a Black American child adopted by a Black American mother. I was back where I started, wading into parenting spaces where all of the mothers' faces were white.

For Black people, trips to the Black bookstore and segregated sections of dying book repositories yielded children's books about grandparents, trickster animals, single parents, books about hope, endurance, family, sports figures, poetry, and music. Some narratives alluded to family configurations with multiple generations sharing a home, but few used the word *adoption*, showed nonrelative caregivers as main characters, or discussed Black people adopting Black children. Once again, the absence of Black parents in adoption literature troubled me. Did I not exist? Were adoption books featuring same-species animals supposed to make Black adoptive parents feel included? What message did adoptive books about children of color send when the parents were always a different race? Would another generation of foster children grow up believing that only white people practiced altruism? Just as I had searched for culturally relevant parenting books, I looked for representations of our life in books I could read to my son. Alas, my cart remained empty.

Back to the library we went.

"Me, again." I smiled. "Do you have any adoption books about Black children who were adopted by Black people?"

The research librarian's fingers flew over the keys. "No, I'm sorry."

"Don't be. I'm used to it."

I took August over to browse the children's book shelves. "Is it me?" I asked him, who blinked and stared at me. "Or is it an intentional omission by the adoption community, which is primarily white?"

The purpose of adoption literature was to build community. Foster/adoptive parents were united in our mission of supporting children in need. We read the same manual and operated from a level playing field of information designed to equip prospective parents, regardless of race, about loss and grief. Children's adoption books were supposed to be inclusive, because we all came face to face with that critical question, *Are you my mother?* But how could I answer that question for August when there were no examples in the adoption canon? If I was erased at the beginning of the conversation, how could I be his anchor and outlet for hard discussions about feeling different for being the only one of color or faith in a small town, high school, church, or neighborhood? How would I normalize his adoption journey if the available literature excluded us? I could have written August a book, except I already wore enough hats and was not about to add that of children's book author. Unwilling to take this erasure lying down, I boycotted white adoption children's stories. Instead, I curated a library with silly stories about ghosts, pumpkins, the Milky Way, and trucks. The answer seemed to be that Black adoptive parents had to be responsible for documenting our own experiences; otherwise we wouldn't even exist in books and the imaginations of white people.

Turning One and Other Milestones

In the absence of adoption parenting books to give me advice on the best way to construct my family, I made our life up as we went along. Five months after he had come to live with me, August was about to turn one. For his first birthday, I forwent a big party. We were still nesting, and I wanted to celebrate our love. I bought August a small cake with white icing and the words *Happy Birthday* written across it in green. I tied a colorful Mylar balloon to his high chair and let him and the dogs make hash of the cake while I sang "Happy Birthday."

We enjoyed our intimate party and prepared to meet our new social worker, Geri. We had not seen nor heard from Renata, and Geri had confirmed we were no longer legally obligated to visit with her, but August's siblings wanted to meet him. I thought that was sweet and agreed to speak with Bria, the foster mother of August's eldest three brothers. After all that I had learned during PS-MAPP training, I was open to getting the kids together. August and his siblings had been deprived of so much. I wanted August to have the richest family life he could and would not keep his siblings from him.

I was surprised by how young Bria was. She couldn't have been more than thirty-five years old, handling her biological son and three additional boys from seventeen to nine, in addition to her job as a teacher's assistant at an elementary school. She was very candid about her struggles trying to raise four boys by herself. Alvin, who was seventeen, kept running away to his father's home thirty miles away. His dad was sick and could not keep him, which was why he was in the system. Wayne was thirteen and Josiah was eleven. Both boys had been physically abused and placed in multiple homes before living with Bria. They had behavior issues and did not listen to her. Malcolm, Bria's biological son, was quiet and seemed younger than his nine years.

Bria was also friends with foster/adoptive mother Ms. Smith. She was older and had adopted Orlando, Ricardo, and Tanya, August's other three siblings. Orlando and Ricardo were half-Mexican and had the same father. Tanya, who was fourteen years old and the second oldest, was the only girl in the group. She was a second mother to all of her brothers. Bria and Ms. Smith regularly got the six siblings together to maintain their bond. I admired their tenacity and agreed to take cupcakes to Ms. Smith's home for a visit. The next Saturday, my cousin Kisha, August, and I pulled up to a white stucco home in Compton, thirty minutes southeast of our home in Beverly Hills. The street was quiet and the house was a good size, though not as nice as Mrs. Wilson's. August didn't know where we were, but I talked to him like he could understand that he would be meeting his siblings.

Unsure of what to expect, I adjusted August's green bib and rang the doorbell, genuinely happy that after today, August would have a relationship with blood relatives. Alvin, Wayne, Josiah, Tanya, Orlando, Ricardo, and Malcolm met us at the door.

"Kemarye is here!" yelled Alvin, taking August from my arms.

Tanya waved. I was taken aback by the use of August's birth name, but I smiled. They did not know I had changed his name, and there was no need to spoil the fun.

"He is so cute!"

"Let me hold him," Tanya said. Alvin was busy tossing August in the air. August was loving it.

"I wanna hold Kemarye," Orlando, who was three, demanded.

We finally made it through the door. August's siblings were overjoyed to meet their baby brother. He soaked up the attention, crawling from lap to lap. Ms. Smith popped out briefly to say hello and then disappeared. Kisha, Bria, and I chatted while the kids loved on their brother.

The kids were clean and friendly, though Ricardo had snot running down his lips. Bria noticed and cleaned his cute face. I kept an eye on August, who still sucked his fingers, secretly praying he did not touch snot and then put his fingers back in his mouth. I did my best not to hover. August was having a good time, and I needed to chill. Over the course of conversation, I learned that

Bria had had several run-ins with Renata, who encouraged the boys to cut school to spend time with her. Renata even told them to ask to be removed from Bria's home. Bria was adamant about keeping the brothers together and willing to weather their angst and Renata's meddling to do so. It was clear that she loved them.

I looked around the wood-paneled living room and felt discouraged. There were no school pictures or toys or anything to suggest that children aged three to fourteen lived there. It was drafty, uninviting, and lacked color, save for the black leather couch and gold picture frame on the wall. This cold room with too many foster children could have been August's life. I was so glad August was mine, safe and thriving with me as his mother.

The kids were anxious to get the party started but Ms. Smith had not returned from wherever she went. Kisha shrugged a couple of times, and I finally asked Bria, "Is she okay?"

"Yeah, I'll get her." Bria was apologetic and went to check on her.

Kisha and I were ready to go, so when Bria came back to the living room, we had gathered the siblings together to sing "Happy Birthday," take pictures, and pass out cupcakes.

Ms. Smith finally joined us. Older and less pleasant than Bria, Ms. Smith talked incessantly about how August would become angry when he turned two years old and that I should let the social worker know. She was insinuating that I could get a larger stipend if I complained that he had anger issues, low-key hinting how to work the system. Ms. Smith's attitude was 180 degrees from Mrs.

Wilson's, August's last foster mother. From this one meeting, she did not seem like the best representation of foster/adoptive single mothers, but I had to remember that she had adopted a sibling set of three when no one else would. I gave her props for that, even though I could tell she thought I was naive for not taking advantage of August's overflowing case file. Our conversation was quickly going downhill. I thanked her for welcoming us into her home and beat a path out the front door. I spoke with Bria a couple more times but never saw her again, closing the door on a life that August escaped.

Bria's stories about Renata's erratic behavior and the precarious situation she was in with the oldest boys helped me make a crucial decision on August's behalf. I had to protect my son. The birthday party was both a success and a deal breaker. August got to meet his biological siblings, but I got the best present: information. Though I was still trying to figure out who August would know as family, the first step would be to notify our social worker that August's adoption would be closed, with no more contact with his biological family.

Before laying eyes on August, I had been willing to accept that biological connections were more powerful than those created through adoption. I bought into suggestions from the PS-MAPP training that a child must know his roots and that foster parents should make every effort to keep those family ties alive. After I met August, however, I could no longer feign ease in linking hands with those whose lifestyle and values were so different from mine.

It wasn't August's siblings' fault that their zip codes denoted drugs, food deserts, storefront churches, gangs, or jail. While there were hard-working families in those neighborhoods, the lure of the streets proved irresistible for too many children and young adults. My family had already witnessed my parents fall through that rabbit hole, and there was no reason to intentionally put August in the crosshairs of a storm he might drown in.

A closed adoption meant that August would be raised with no contact with his siblings or other biological relatives. I didn't want him to feel better than his brothers and sister because of the opportunities he would have, or less than because they had each other and he was alone. There was too much at stake, and one unsupervised weekend could change the course of his life. I couldn't have that. August was going places. He would be free to step into his new identity and engage the world unencumbered by the circumstances of his birth.

With the belief that I was doing what was best for August, I requested that our records be sealed. I was willing to risk August's future anger for denying him access to his biological family. He would have to trust my judgment and rely on the photo album I assembled with their pictures for a connection. When he became an adult, I would help him find his people, if that was what he wanted.

The Obama Season

One year after deciding to close August's adoption, I was still happy about my decision to check *boy* on the placement paperwork. I loved having a son and thought I understood what it meant to raise a little Black boy—until I actually saw a Black man work hard and become president of the United States. Obama was a living and breathing example of what a great education could yield. He was the manifestation of my hopes and dreams for my son. Because I wanted this great good for August, I had to interrogate how I viewed the world. I was tasked with shaping my baby into a person, and excited that he had been born the year before America elected its first Black president.

My grandparents were ecstatic about Obama's victory. Henry, who had been a conservative Democrat, purchased memorabilia and hung a poster of the First Family in the foyer of the house. He also bought commemorative plates and multiple newspapers with different headlines that all said the same thing: a Black man was now in charge.

As excited as I was about Obama's presidency, I was even more gratified that my grandparents lived to see that historic victory. A Black man's ascendance to the American throne suggested our nation's coming of age in race relations and a bursting pride amongst the grandchildren of slaves, immigrants, people of all colors, creeds, and religious beliefs, and single mothers raising boys. He made me proud to be an American, and I felt a renewed responsibility for the gift of my then twenty-two-month-old son, who sported a U.S. flag–inspired tee with FUTURE PRESIDENT stamped across his chest that fateful night in 2008.

I took August to Obama's first inauguration in Washington, DC, though the day Senator Barack Obama was sworn in as president, we stayed inside. It was too cold and too crowded to navigate August's stroller among hundreds of thousands of well-wishers, but we met my friends Rudy and Marguerite on the Capitol Mall afterward.

"Hey, man!" Rudy took August out of his stroller and spun him around. There was nothing but trash and vendors left once the throngs of supporters were gone. It didn't matter. The shift in the air was real. The atmosphere was euphoric and overflowing with people from all over the world, and Black pride was everywhere.

"Did you watch it?" Marguerite asked, rubbing August's arms.

"Every single minute."

"White folks have been real friendly." Rudy laughed. "Today, we were all one nation, indivisible, with liberty and justice for all."

"It won't last, but I'll take it," Marguerite said.

What a heady way to begin the year, and 2009 would soon bring even more joy. August's adoption would be finalized in June. I couldn't wait! On the plane ride home, I reflected on the promise of what America owed us. Obama's election made the American dream a reality for my son, and I wanted to harness every morsel of it so I could give it to August as he grew from boy to man.

I remembered debating with Henry and Dr. McIver, my older esteemed, Black Republican doctor, about the chances of a Black man becoming the leader of the free world. I was confident it would happen in my lifetime and hoped reparations would follow shortly thereafter. Of all the candidates who tossed their hats in the race, though, I was relieved when a real person won the nomination. Barack Obama was like people I knew. He was raised by a single mom and grandparents, endured prejudice as a child at the prep high school he attended, and was made to understand that as a Black man in America, white people would underestimate him. Because he was biracial, Black people would want to know which team he played for and challenge his love for Black folks. As Obama wrote in his memoir, *Dreams from My Father: A Story of Race and Inheritance*, he lost his way for a short while and then got himself together when he transferred to Columbia University. Handsome, with the ability to code switch between white and Black worlds, and a Harvard Law School graduate,

Obama had all of the trappings of success. He was palatable across most racial groups with a guaranteed pass to thrive among whites. And yet, he resisted being the token in the room, where he would be rewarded if he rejected his Blackness. Obama took community service seriously and gave back, not because he had to, but because he wanted to. He gave me, a single Black adoptive mother, a tangible image of a Black man for August to aspire to be. No disrespect to Dr. King, Malcolm X, or Frederick Douglass, but my son needed a living, breathing, imperfect man raised by a single mother to see the possibility for his life. And without a man in the house for August to see shaving or cooking or getting dressed for work each day, Obama became my go-to.

To anyone else, it may have seemed obvious who I would cast my vote for in 2008. But it wasn't that easy. I held strong opinions about uplifting my race, having listened to my father go on and on about white people. But I was also a feminist who knew the history of Black women who were used by the civil rights and Black Power movements and held equally strong feelings about Black men automatically assuming Black women should have their backs, without reciprocity. There were unpunished crimes committed against Black women and girls that needed address-ing, and Black men needed to raise their voices in support of their Black queens. Black women suffered from depression and post-traumatic stress disorder (PTSD) in the worst way, and without a room of our own, we would perish.

The entire preelection cycle sent me sorting through these

contradictions, which originated during the conversations over family holiday dinners when I was a child. There were so many things I wanted to share with August about the importance of beginning his life draped in hope, and early in 2009 I wrote him a letter with the hope that one day he would be able to read it and understand why this time in history was so important to me and others in our community.

March 1, 2009

Dear August,

Up until now, my views on race and gender were academic. I have long known the facts of racism in America. I am a historian and didn't expect America to fulfill most of its promises. Becoming a mother forced me to have hope. Obama was at least someone I could trust to try to make the world better and safer for my child. You won't remember our trip to Washington, DC, but I took you so that you could see what America owed you. I felt renewed and then took you on a bumpy philosophical excursion down memory lane through my actual understanding of when and where I enter and when and where you will enter when you become a man.

My political understanding began at the dining room table. After holiday dinners, Grandpa Henry, Uncle Roy, and Cousin Ray usually sat at one table while Grandma Ann, Aunt Ethel, Aunt Helen, and my mother, if she was in town, sat at another. I sat at the kids' table or with the men. I joined their conversations about current events, travel, and whatever hot political topics I learned from the news or at school. It was as natural for me to join this space as girls who sat under their mothers. I was a tomboy and felt confident in this authentic Black male sphere. The men saw me as a fully formed human being, and no one told me I had stepped out of my place. Nor was there an expectation that I sit in the company of women or pick up traditional feminine attributes. Black maleness was a positive experience for me and provided context for my adoption of a baby boy.

My first inkling that something was wrong with my blanket acceptance of all things Black male was foisted upon me when I shunned my gender and supported Clarence Thomas's nomination to the U.S. Supreme Court. It was a reluctant endorsement, because I knew Anita Hill was telling the truth. It was brave of her to come forward about being sexually harassed by a man in power. Misguidedly, I thought that Thomas should be confirmed because it would be decades before another Black person sat on the highest court in the land. In short, I put my race first. Fresh out of undergrad school, I still equated race with men. That was what I missed on family holidays when the sexes separated after dinner. I saw myself as bridging a divide, because I did not understand my intersectional experience. I grew up thinking that race took precedence over gender. No one told me that but it was in all of the messaging. Rosa Parks was a tired woman, not a committed activist and secretary for the NAACP in Birmingham, Alabama, long before Martin and his family moved to the area. Dr. King was the face of the civil rights movement, the speech he wrote about the bounced check America wrote to its Black citizens would not be memorable had gospel singer Mahalia Jackson, sitting behind him on the dais, not encouraged him to go off script and talk about his dream.

In 1994, I entered graduate school, where my real political awakening transpired. Through the study of Professor Kimberlé Crenshaw's intersectionality, I realized my mistake: Clarence Thomas's alleged deeds nullified his place, our place, on the U.S. Supreme Court. Period. In the parlance of an intersectional discourse, I had prefaced race, read: men over gender, read: woman. Not to excuse my ignorance, but I thought that loyalty within communities of color was genetic, stemming from slavery and the powerlessness it imbued in Black men to protect their families. There was also the undeniable legacy of the Jim Crow era, white male privilege, and the patriarchal mindset of a country built on greed, oppression, theft, and violence that disenfranchised generations of Black men. Women, (read: white women) had an entire movement dedicated to advancing their needs, not mine. Black women lived at the intersection of race and gender, and these two immutable factors were directly impacted by education, class, and in my case, motherhood. An educated, single mother, who was middle class and heterosexual, I was supposed to live at the margins of society. My class and education level disrupted the myth of the Black welfare queen, and I felt empowered to go where I pleased and take any route to parenthood I saw fit.

White America may have regarded single Black mothers as inter-sectionally invisible and read women as white, but we knew our worth as intrinsic contributors to the fabric of this country. There was no United States of America without Black mothers.

With new priorities in order—a man should not get a pass just because he was Black—I viewed the Million Man March of 1995 as sexist and exclusionary. Given the blood, sweat, and babies born for the revolution, I saw it as a double setback for my race and my gender. How could men come together to discuss the Black family without women? It was a monologue when it should have been a dialogue. A dialogue between equals. I snubbed the women who supported this march as unenlightened and enablers of male chauvinism. What was wrong with them? Didn't they recognize this as a throwback to the 1940s, '50s, '60s, and '70s when Black men took all the glory for shouldering the race while women did the heavy lifting? Couldn't they see that men were putting themselves first (again) and expecting us to sit home and wait for them to tell us what to do? I had become a feminist who was shut out by men. That experience was jarring.

In 2008, a Black man faced off with a white woman for the Oval Office. What would I do? More mature and socially astute than the twenty-year-old version of myself, I was no longer racially blind, and had Senator Obama been accused of scandalous behavior like Clarence Thomas, I would've voted for Hillary. I did think that if Obama missed this opportunity, Black folks might have a long wait for the brass ring. This time, I was willing to risk it. I had become an adjunct U.S. history professor trained in distancing myself from the pain and horror of our Black genocide. But I was also a mother, desperate for change. I needed the right role model. You needed the right role model. Not just any Black man would have the privilege of being one of your heroes. I had standards and a short list of undesirable candidates I would never endorse. Larry Elder confused me. I could not tell which team he was on. Former GOP Chairman Michael Steele allowed Rush Limbaugh to punk him. For all of his education and political experience, he did not seem like his own man and Ward Connerly...don't get me started. So, here's where the lie enters the scenario: My earlier support of Thomas was based on the idea that I had to vote for a Black man because he was Black. Barack Obama's candidacy freed me from that knee-jerk tendency to support my race without critically considering their qualifications, integrity, political philosophies, and professional track records. Blackness, my conflicted intersectional feminism finally understood, would be the capstone, not the center.

Freed from uninterrogated loyalty, I stepped back and assessed Obama's bid for the presidency in concrete terms. I agreed with his stances on the war in Iraq, healthcare, and energy reforms. I admired his decision to work as a community organizer, rather than at a large law firm where he would have made partner and earned a six-figure income. Now, that was cool! I considered America's free-falling international reputation, and saw Obama as possessing the best ability to raise our profile abroad. Much like President Bill Clinton, Senator Obama had the "it" factor that cut across race, sexuality, nationality, and religion. And finally, his stroll was replete with swag and the nod.

Ironically, your adoption placement and Obama's ascendance to the throne resurrected that old feeling of being able to navigate any space, traditionally white female or Black male, I wanted. Even the lack of culturally relevant parenting information for Black parents and mainstream feminists who kept trying to keep Black women at the bottom of the race/gender hierarchy or Black men who questioned my ability to raise a boy solo could not steal my happiness. I was a proud mom, and you were my son. It was a zeitgeist.

Obama's win gave Black people certainty that every lynching, cross burning, mandatory minimum sentence, rape, economic setback, unsafe neighborhood, and impoverished community led to this moment. That the price we paid to get a Black man elected as the forty-fourth president of the United States was worth it. "The president justified the faith of generations who persisted in loving America—even when the nation refused to love us back." (I stole that quote from Dr. Peniel E. Joseph.) As a single Black mother, I felt renewed. I could strut about the country, knowing that where society saw a Black welfare queen, I saw the mother of a future president. No pressure. LOL.

Love,

Mommy

Rituals and Rites of Passage

June 1, 2009. The day had finally arrived. In a couple of hours, August and I would legally be mother and son. Rather than wait for National Adoption Day in November, where a public adoption attorney would be assigned to our case, I shelled out four hundred dollars for a private adoption attorney. I was eager to get the show on the road and willing to wait four weeks for the County to reimburse my legal fees. We had endured nine social workers, attended birth mother visits with Renata, met August's siblings, and witnessed Barack Obama become president of the United States. It was time to close this chapter on the process of becoming a forever family and move forward.

"Good morning, angel," I sang. "Guess what today is?"

"My burfday?" he said through toothpaste bubbles.

"No, silly goose. Today is the day that I get to adopt you." I wiped his mouth.

"And then I get a train?" August was trying to twist past me.

I pretended to be exasperated. "Is that all you ever think about?"

August had slipped through my grasp. I chased him and covered his brown tummy with kisses. Baby fat slowly disappearing, my once pudgy two-and-a-half-year-old was stretching into a real little boy.

"We have to pick up Grandma Ann. Get dressed." I had laid his outfit out the night before. We started with Elmo Pull-Ups and ended with black loafers, a white button-down shirt, black pants, and a powder-blue, gray, and yellow argyle vest. I matched August's outfit with a navy-blue cashmere sweater and gray slacks. We looked good. I felt a quiet excitement. In less than two years, August had gone from special ops crawling to running, speaking, and naming the planets in the solar system. He was everything, and more than I could've dreamt of.

Ann was ready in a speckled gray blazer and burgundy pants. "Is Helen riding with us?"

"No, we'll meet her at the courthouse."

Several of my friends had taken the day off work to join us in Judge Redmond's chambers. The judge was a friend of mine and agreed to officiate for us. Our attorney and his assistant met us outside the courtroom. I had to sign the adoption order and adoption agreement, which he would submit to the judge for her signature. These documents would receive an embossed stamp with the seal of California and be mailed to me at a later date.

There were several families becoming forever families that

day. Kids were running around and August joined them. We made small talk with a large Latinx family during the two hours we waited for our case number to be called. August, Lori, Kisha, Hazyl, Tricia, Ann, Helen, Nedra, our attorney, and I filed into the wood-paneled room. August, Lori, Helen, and I took our seats at the long table. There was a court reporter and three other court staff waiting for us. August had his choice of teddy bears and chose the blue one. While Judge Redmond spoke to me, August played with the bear. Judge Redmond told me that August would receive a new birth certificate with my name listed in the mother-of-child box. She wrapped up the twenty-minute preceding by presenting us with a certificate: "On behalf of the Superior Court of the great State of California, August Sebastian Austin is now and forever a member of the Austin family." Everyone cheered.

Finally, I had graduated into official motherhood.

———————

The finalization of August's adoption was one of the best days of my life. I had survived family judgment and negative stereotypes by mainstream society, found the best resources I could to support my journey, and made my own way in a world that was largely foreign to me and my community. But then a month later an ugly, unbalanced article appeared on CNN's website. "Single Black Women Choosing to Adopt" by John Blake relied on a trite assumption that there were no Black men for Black women to marry because they were either gay or in jail, and thus no one with whom to procreate. Blake suggested that single Black women who wanted to become mothers had only one choice, and that was adoption. Our intersectional invisibility made it impossible for him to imagine a Black woman using a surrogate, in vitro fertilization (IVF), a sperm donor, or any other potential path to motherhood.

Wendy, the subject of the article, was a Black woman who was venting about her specific dating woes. Wendy did not speak for nor represent all of us. Blake's reporting was lazy and lacked an alternate perspective. Not every Black woman was upset about not having a man, and, in fact, there was a myriad of reasons single women adopted. Had he asked me, I would have shared that the mommie-jones wore me down. I would have explained that the timing was right and that my intersectional experience as a Black woman mixed with a special brand of conflicted feminism and a desire to pay it forward sent me out the door to the foster/adoption orientation in September 2006.

Blake did what mainstream media typically did to communities of color: affixed a label and then left us holding a bag filled with scandalous statistics, half-truths, and self-loathing. The point of that article should have been that a particular woman was so disturbed by her lack of dating prospects that she decided to adopt a child. Despite operating under the unconscious grip of a paternalistic society and thinking she needed a man to complete her, her actual objective was motherhood. As horrified as I was by the article and Wendy's willingness to put her dreams of motherhood on hold waiting for the ideal Black man, I understood her think-ing. She was putting the race first, not realizing that she did not need masculine permission to become a mom.

Without many resources, I had figured out this mothering thing, but the stereotypes and foolishness were still out in the world without many positive images of alternate lifestyles to combat them.

Everybody Has an Opinion

Now that I was officially August's mother, I thought I would be free to parent him as I chose. It turns out that everybody had an opinion. Not only was my identity of single Black mother being confronted by the media, I started feeling pressure from friends to take August to church. A public religious commitment was deemed essential in the Black community, and being a single mother of a Black boy escalated other people's opinion that I *had to have that boy in church*. I believed in God but didn't see a reason to go to an actual church. No one pestered me about it when I was on my own, but after I became a mom, the expectation that August needed a formal religious upbringing was something I faced constantly. Rudy, now August's godfather, and Marguerite asked about it several times after the finalization of his adoption.

"This isn't about you. You already have a belief system. August needs one," Marguerite advised.

I valued their opinions and their early support of my decision to adopt. When other folks laughed or thought I was joking, they had encouraged me. Rudy was one of the first to declare his love of August and treated him like family immediately.

Ironically, my faithful Methodist and Baptist grandparents did not press me about religion. They knew I was a heathen with a big heart. I grew up in a church where we did not shout Amen, dance in the aisle, or rock our bodies to soulful music. We politely clapped and listened attentively to the sermon and announcements. As much as I liked our church, it was boring—not that the lively Baptist tabernacle of Grandma's was any better.

In my early forties, I still snickered during shrill choir solos performed by tone-deaf octogenarians and refused to support Samaritans perched outside grocery stores asking for coins to save homeless children. Always one for a good conspiracy theory, I'm open to the possibility that Mary Magdalene's image was erased from Leonardo da Vinci's *The Last Supper*. I have dipped, kneeled, and crossed myself in Catholic vestibules and arrived bare-legged to church services. I had no idea how many books were in the Bible and believed that playing small to please others was just as sinful as not sharing one's gifts. I was bothered by feminine portrayals of women as harlots or long-suffering saints and hard-pressed to believe that Jesus was blond and blue-eyed. Mrs. Wilson, August's last foster mother, would have run me out of her home if she knew my true feelings, which was why I kept my blasphemous opinions to myself during the visit that led to me becoming August's mother.

My spiritual guides included Deepak Chopra, Florence Scovel

Shinn, the über-positive Joel Osteen, and peripatetic Bishop T. D. Jakes. Referring to the same Bible I came of age on, those humans preached oneness with God, forgiveness, and abundance, minus all the withering judgment famously found in the *good book*. As an adult, I practiced a hybrid of Judeo-Christianity, Eastern philosophy, and positive affirmations. All of this was fine for me, but as August grew from toddler to snaggle-toothed kindergartener, I began feeling conflicted about how to shape his understanding of a power greater than himself. The pressure to instill a sense of wonder of the physical earth and mankind's generosity and shortcomings through spirituality was immense. He would believe whatever I told him, and that was scary. Without a partner with whom to share or combine beliefs about the world and our place in it, I tempered my critique of Christianity with the goal of raising a child open to finding the good in all theology.

In the throes of sorting through how to decode Christianity for him, I taught August my childhood prayer: "Now I lay me down to sleep, I pray the Lord my soul to keep. If I should die before I awake, I pray the Lord my soul to take. In Jesus's name. Amen." From there we blessed red bear, Grandma Ann, other relatives, Nancy, and his teachers. Raspberries planted on cheeks, a deluge of sweet kisses, and then *I love you*s followed my exit from his room each night. This prayer signaled that no matter what happened during the day, he was always safe and divinely protected. There were a few declarative statements in the Lord's Prayer I liked, so I taught him that one too.

I stalled our church attendance as long as I could. Then, as the finalization of August's adoption loomed, my sassy friend Hazyl asked if I was going to have him christened. Prior to her asking, I had not thought about it. *Do I have to?* I wondered. I already felt blessed. All of the stars had aligned to bring August into my life, and I relished being a mom. The wrinkles in the two-year dealings with the County were over, and I was conquering motherhood one issue at a time. Given my obvious distrust of Christianity, having August christened seemed hypocritical. I justified my actions because I was two years into my parenting gig and still applying finishing touches to things single adoptive parents did to fit in. There were so many spaces where single Black mothers and their children were ignored, erased, or demeaned that I felt compelled to step outside my comfort zone to normalize our union in the eyes of others.

I wanted August to be included in this particular rite of passage. "You know we don't have a church home."

"Not a problem; my pastor will do it," Hazyl confirmed.

"But we're not Presbyterian."

"Not a problem," she said again. "I got you."

"All right," I said to Hazyl, and everyone else quickly was on board. Soon an Evite, decorated with August's smiling face and the text of Ephesians 1:5: "In love, he destined us for adoption," went out to family and friends.

Dapper August, dressed in a white christening jumpsuit with matching cap, and I, in pearls, stood at the altar and received

God's blessing. The service was short, with Rudy, godmother Lori, and I promising to seek God's counsel on all matters large and small, and me repeating a few vows. The female pastor dipped her right finger in holy water and drew a cross on August's forehead. August's soul was officially washed white as snow, and I, the prodigal daughter, was admonished to go and sin no more.

August's christening was our little family's public announcement that we respected traditional cultural rituals and planned to be part of the community. But I would not teach August that Jesus was white, nor show him the ubiquitous photo of the blue-eyed, sandy blond with the pious expression. This was not a rejection of Jesus, whom I believed walked the earth—it was rejection of the image of white as good, pure, clean, and the absence of color as dark and evil. As a child, I thought the Bible was the gospel and believed every stereotype about white being right and dark being bad. It wasn't fair to teach children of color that a man from the Middle East looked European or that my skin color, which I had no control over, destined me to be less than the white person seated next to me. August would suffer through that mess in English literature when he got older, and there was no point in starting him off thinking he was born in sin.

Luckily, I had not been subjected to a picture of white Jesus growing up, but I had friends whose grandmas proudly mounted the holy trinity—Jesus, Dr. Martin Luther King Jr., and President John F. Kennedy over their fireplaces. Jesus was *the truth, the way, and the light,* Dr. King was assassinated for his dream to come to fruition, and JFK sent troops to enforce desegregation in the South. All three men had been murdered to advance the human race, and many older Black people had not forgotten their sacrifices. My parents' generation saw things a little differently. Those who remained in the Christian church joined progressive or Afrocentric churches that reimagined Jesus with dark skin, full lips, and a broad nose. This was their way of leveling the Christian playing field and making people feel good about pleasing a man who looked like them.

I simply decided that there were too many scriptures supporting racial hierarchy, and as a modern parent, I would not saddle August with an inferiority complex. Black people were allegedly descended from Canaan, whose grandfather Noah cursed him. The oversimplifed version is that Ham, father of Canaan, told his brothers that their father, Noah, was passed out drunk and naked. Feeling disrespected, Noah declared that all of Canaan's descendants would be servants. Slave owners ran with this interpretation and used it to justify the enslavement of Africans as the natural order of things. I would not allow August to grow up thinking that Black people had only ever lived at the bottom of society.

He would also never see Charlton Heston as Moses in *The Ten Commandments*. The powerful cinematography was captivating and promoted a vengeful God from the Old Testament. I was a New Testament kind of gal and was taught that our God was a forgiving God, so I would pass that belief on to August. In the movie, the narrator's overly dramatic authoritative tone combined with theatrical music gave the impression that the featured events really happened in the way producer Cecil B. DeMille said they did. I did not believe that Moses raised a staff and parted 190 miles of Red Sea. I was more inclined to embrace the religious science rumination that Moses's faith and courage gave him the fortitude to cross several figurative Red Seas, including escaping the Egyptians and surmounting the fears of his own people. I too have crossed Red Seas. One was the decision whether to have an open or closed adoption.

With the trappings of organized religion off the table, I allowed August to experience different types of religious practices. He attended Catholic Church with Cousin Ray and Shabbat at the neighbors'. I thought it was cool he was learning there was more than one way to worship God. When August outgrew Nancy's in-home day care, he attended the local Montessori school, which was expensive and predominantly white. Religion was not an issue there, and Maria Montessori's child-centered philosophy would be a good fit for August, who could preread and do simple arithmetic. But when his teacher quit, I switched him to the Walton's Wiz Kids, a purportedly non-Christian, predominantly Black school, where the founder was known to produce highly gifted children. Almost immediately, we had a problem. The students at Walton's Wiz Kids prayed before lunch, and August came home talking about how Jesus would help him make his bed.

I indulged the premeal prayer but found it difficult to refrain from correcting his assertion that Jesus would do his chores, if only he asked. The secular truth was that God helped those who helped themselves, and August had to learn to seek solutions, not wait for someone else to save him. I was upset he was being taught the same nonsense, paralytic Christianity I had learned as a child. I contemplated starting August off with a lesson in quantum physics—what he put his energy on would be drawn to him. It was an interesting strategy, but the possibility of him rejecting all spirituality was not my goal either. What I wanted was to blend Christian principles like charity and grace with ideals of hard work and personal accountability to give him a solid grounding.

There were churches that offered the type of teaching I was looking for, but that meant I had to actually get us in the car and then drive there. After working all week and mothering solo, my excuse was that I was tired. The thought of doing one more thing, even church, was not attractive. And while I may have scored points for adopting a child, I was not a good Christian. We pretty much went to church for special occasions or events. That's all I could stomach.

Ultimately, I chose to teach August that heaven and hell were not postmortem destinations. I had experienced both and wanted him to know that life, the one he was presently living, would be filled with both ecstasy and purgatory. My favorite life commandment was Karma 101—do unto others as he would have others do unto him. As he grew older, I would instruct him to trust his intuition, to be positive, and that failure was a great teacher. I would tell him that God lived in his heart and, kind of like Santa

Claus, knew his every thought and desire. I was determined that his actions would match his character. Pretending to be a "good boy" as per external definitions, was a trick bag that would tamper with his integrity and teach him to be honest but insincere. August needed to be clear on his intentions, be of service to others, and enjoy the journey of his life. Those were not traditional Christian commandments, but they were attainable goals.

Motherhood entailed so many decisions. Who knew? Even with my official paperwork complete, I was still learning.

Got My Sea Legs

In the spirit of service, I agreed to an invitation from August's first social worker, Donna, to publicly share my adoption experience. She was running the same PS-MAPP training I had taken and needed a resource parent to be honest with prospective foster/adoptive parents about the process and what their expectations should be.

"Nef, please bring August. The families need to see that adoption can really happen. Oh, and bring your photo album or scrapbook with pictures."

"Okay. Um, I never got around to making a photo album." I laughed. "There's just not enough time in the day. I can hardly believe he is already three."

"That's amazing. Has it been that long?"

"I do have a DVD of his life from the day we met through the finalization of his adoption. Can I bring that instead?"

"That will be perfect. See you next week."

"Three years ago, I sat where you are, excited and nervous about becoming a first-time mom through adoption. The process was more than I bargained for, but as you can see"—I pointed to August—"it was time well spent." I launched into my foster/adoption experience of two attempted placements before meeting August, birth mother visits, nine social workers, and no birth certificate. I explained how I handled my family's reaction to the news that I was going to adopt, and how my life changed completely for the better. As I spoke, I scanned the participants to see how many single foster/adoptive parents were in the room. There was one.

I intentionally maintained eye contact with the single Black woman, telepathically letting her know that no matter how challenging the process became, she would make it to the other side. I wondered if she too had tried to research single Black adoptive mothers and come up empty-handed. I approached her after class and told her to stay strong.

That was the first of many presentations I gave. I really enjoyed speaking with prospective foster/adoptive families and considered starting a blog, but I was hesitant to reveal too much about myself online and wasn't sure how many people would actually be interested in reading my ramblings. I hated the idea of oversharing but could not deny how easy it was to find information about almost all parenting models except mine, and that I could do something to remedy that problem. There were thousands of Black children in foster care, and there had to be a way to connect with my sisters considering alternative paths to parenthood, but I kept meeting women who did not want to go the public adoption route. They turned their professional noses up at the County, believing the smear campaign and horror stories about foster children in the local paper.

Those who might have been willing to brave DCFS were afraid to take next steps. The reasons varied, but mostly fell into four categories: fear that all of the children in foster care were damaged; uncertainty about adopting a child they did not know; holding out for a husband, because they did not want to be the proverbial single Black mother; or they thought it was expensive to adopt. None of the women I spoke with knew a single Black woman who had successfully adopted solo, and assumed those who had had thousands of dollars in savings and owned a home—until they met me.

I was able to tell them there was no magic involved in adopting a child. I did not have special favor, and if I could do it, there was hope yet for them. If a 2007 *New York Times* article was accurate and 70 percent of Black women were currently single, and half of that number had children, then the group currently without children was best situated to adopt. Black children comprised 30 percent of the nationwide total of 423,773 children in foster care. What a difference we could make in the lives of these children, our children, if only we knew we could. I was becoming an adoption ambassador to strangers and to my childless friends, who were charmed by August. In his eyes, they saw a future for themselves.

I had finally gotten my parenting sea legs and felt competent in my role as August's mother. Even after I became a mom, I only heard from my mother, Diane, once or twice per month. She felt that since August couldn't talk, there was no point in calling all the time. Though she tried to make up for this by being the doting grandma when she was in town, it was still mind-boggling that she didn't call more. Ann called every single day after August was placed with me. My slobbering baby boy would pant heavily into the receiver. He knew Great Grandma's voice and perked up when she called. Ann always asked how I was doing and what August was up to that day. The phone calls, along with money, meals, and parenting advice were Ann's way of showing up and being supportive.

I was still teaching at the college and wanting to advance the cause for domestic adoption. Specifically, I wanted to give single Black women more tangible examples of what single adoption looked like. So, I finally decided to start a blog and scoured the internet for first-person testimonials written by Black women who had adopted. I reposted an essay, "In the Absence of Blood" written by adoptive mom Kim Green. She was an adoptee herself from the projects in Cincinnati. The area was rife with tired women raising fatherless children, and the men in her family were absent and unconcerned. Ms. Green did not want to repeat that cycle, nor subject her body to the dichotomous joys and horrors of pregnancy. Even as a child, she knew she would adopt someday, and did so in her late thirties. Kim's story was moving, and I sent it straight to my friends who had hinted that they too wanted to adopt.

I was trying to find the best balance of Black adoption stories with parenting information to post on my blog when I saw *Mother and Child* by Rodrigo García. Art imitated life in the film, which linked three women through adoption. One character gave her child up for adoption after becoming pregnant at fourteen; another didn't think she could have children; and a third was married but unable to conceive. The latter couple, who were Black, caught my eye. It was a rarity to see people of color deal with infertility on the big or small screen. Those were real issues in our community that needed the light of day. They chose adoption and their respective middle-class families were unsupportive. They were suspicious of the adoption process and advised them not to adopt a child they did not know. Steadfast, the couple moved forward with their plan. Both Kim and the fictional couple achieved their dream of parenthood through adoption. They did not allow society, family, or myth to dictate how they created their families. Their stories set the tone for my blog.

More than one friend commented that I made parenting look easy, but part of the reason I was exploring on my blog how Black women were faring as mothers was because I was feeling the weight of trying to do everything by myself. Most days, I was in survival mode, stuck on the hamster wheel of rising early, walking the dogs, getting August ready for school, dropping him off, going to work, picking him up, spending time with family who lived way across town, cooking dinner, cleaning my apartment, walking the dogs again, going to bed, and then doing it all over again the next day. I had our schedule down to a science, but it came at a cost. I barely recognized myself and had what Dr. Maya Angelou described as "a kind of strength that was almost frightening."

I wasn't the only one running this race. Lori had three kids, my sorority sister Lisa had two, and they were both married. I watched them juggle full-time jobs, manage their homes, spouses, office politics, assist their parents, and put in volunteer hours at their kids' schools. I was now a member of that mother club, with lots of simultaneous moving parts with no time to whine about being tired or stressed or on the verge of losing it. Sometimes our conversations began and ended with, "Girl, you know I know." Mothering was all-encompassing, and single mothering happened at warp speed.

Building My Village

I was on a roll. Mothering, blogging, speaking at PS-MAPP training classes, and recovering some semblance of a social life. I also had my eye on a dude. Richard and I had known each other for over a decade but had not seen each other in a long while. Nursing a broken heart, I had missed an opportunity with him years before. We lost contact and then ran into each other at a mutual friend's house. By then, I had become a mom and he had started his own law practice. Richard was cute, handy with tools, and an adoptee—a trifecta in my book. Without prompting, he brought four-year-old August small race cars and easily engaged him. I watched them play together and thought, *maybe*.

August and I had been together nearly nonstop for his entire life. We had celebrated three Mother's Days and each had gone off without a hitch. August never let on that he missed Renata, though twice he told me I was not his mother. He was riding his scooter and didn't want to stop. It was getting dark, and he needed to eat dinner and take a bath. August looked me in my eyes and announced, "You're not my mother. I don't have to." I congratulated him on knowing I was not his mother and joked that when he saw her that he should tell her she owed me some money. Our standoff was short-lived. August got off the scooter and went inside.

August and I were very close, but our bond was tested on the third Father's Day we spent together. Most of the kids at the Montessori preschool August attended lived in two-parent homes. The few who did not saw their fathers midweek and on the weekends. August was the only adoptee in his class and the only child without a father in the home or in his life. As Father's Day approached, commercials thanking dads and close-up pictures of smiling fathers and sons appeared on TV. I could see the wheels spinning in August's head. Those happy images did not mirror his life with a single mother. When he asked where his dad was, I was honest and told him I did not know. All I had was a name, photo, and place of birth. I had to dig deep to give August a connection. "You get your height, long legs, and arms from your parents," I announced on multiple occasions. His questions let me know that August was thinking about his heritage. Because August and I were both bibliophiles with freckles across our noses, I kept forgetting he was adopted. I'd have to do a better job of keeping the idea of his dad present in our lives.

Though August took the information I provided in stride, the question of who and where his father was would come up again.

Those concerns dogged single mothers' steps around Father's Day and family tree projects, but did not arise for couples. Women who used sperm donors had genetic and biographical details about their donor and could share the donor's profession, hobbies, and health report with their children. This information was required, even if a donor chose to remain anonymous. Surrogates were fully equipped with the biological mother's eggs and/or the father's semen. Though the mother did not carry the baby in her womb, there was a biological connection between one or both parents. Nonrelative adopted children like August had no blood ties to their adoptive parents. I wished I could tell him that his love of trains came from his dad or that all the men in the family had flat feet, but I couldn't know for sure. I had so little to share.

The kids at preschool made ties from blue cardboard and decorated rocks to present to their fathers. I alerted Rudy in advance, and he agreed to go to the Father's Day assembly. I also told August's preschool teacher Ms. Rona, so that she could refer to August's godfather and not his father. She knew he was adopted and agreed to help me normalize this event for August. We were like the majority of households in America, headed by a single mother, but this was small consolation for August. I attempted damage control and told August that Uncle Rudy would be at the assembly. August was happy and addressed his gift accordingly. On the day of the event, Ms. Rona called. She said that August was rolling around on the floor, crying, "I don't have a dad. I don't have a dad."

My heart broke. Though August knew he was adopted, the

realization that our family dynamic was different from his peers must have set in as the fathers arrived to sit with their children. I imagined August's lips trembling and tears streaming down his face, knowing that he would not be one of the preschoolers shouting, "Daddy, Daddy, look what I made," with glee.

His reaction surprised me. I had no idea how strongly August missed a man he had never met. I had grown up with a father and always had Henry, so I had nothing in my arsenal to prepare either one of us for the emptiness a child might feel on such an occasion. I had underestimated the power of loss and realized for the first time that August was holding a place in his heart for his father. If I could have conjured up a dad, I would have. Instead, I did the next best thing—I asked my coworkers Tommy and Terrance to meet Rudy at August's school, explaining that he needed extra support. Both men stopped what they were doing and left the office. I stayed behind, white-knuckling the urge to rush to August and wipe his tears. My presence would have made the situation worse. He would have seen me and boo-hooed harder. That would have elicited pity from the other parents, and August deserved better than that. Later, Rudy told me that once August saw him, he was fine. Tommy and Terrance confirmed what Rudy said. That night, I squeezed my little guy tight. In all of our time together, that was our lowest moment. I was sorry that not having a father on Father's Day sucked, but it was what it was. What August *did* have was a male community that showed up for him when he needed them.

The next year, I began talking with August about Father's Day early. There would be no meltdown, no feeling sorry for himself. I had moved him to Walton's Wiz Kids, and they followed a different school calendar. The school year ended two weeks before Father's Day, so there was no assembly to worry about. What a difference a year made. August was happy to give his godfather a gift, and we spent time with Henry. By the time August entered kindergarten, he was able to articulate that he was adopted and lived with his mom. He told his classmates that everyone had a mother and father, and it happened that he did not know his. August spoke his truth matter-of-factly, and his buddy John told him that he'd share his dad, Coach Tony, with him. Once again, the male community came through for us.

———————

Before August went to the local Montessori preschool, Nancy had begun potty training all of the toddlers at day care. I mimicked what she did at home. We started with a two-tone green frog potty with urine guard, so pee would not overshoot the top and wet the floor. After taking it apart and reassembling it, August would sit and watch *Sesame Street*. I was fine with dumping his urine, but bowel movements that smelled like big-kid poop were too gross. After one particularly large BM, I moved August to the toilet with an Elmo potty seat. A few weeks into potty training, I was waiting for August at Nancy's. We were headed home, and he had to grab his Spider-Man backpack. Jada and Kelly, his day-care buddies, were waiting for their parents. Nancy and I were shooting the shit, and Kelly told Nancy she had to use the bathroom. She and Jada had mastered the potty, while August and the other three-year-old boy, Dane, were still happily wearing Pull-Ups. That gave me an idea. I presented August with a pair of Elmo underwear and told him that if his Pull-Up remained dry and he peed in the toilet, he could wear them. August aced the challenge, and I was finished with the diaper/Pull-Up/baby food aisle at the grocery store and Target forever.

After that, we had a new milestone to achieve because August sat when he urinated. There were ways to teach him how to pee standing up, but the best option was for him to learn from imitating a man. That posed a bit of a problem, because the only male who lived with us was my eleven-year-old dog, LL Cool J. LL knew how to lift his leg, which I witnessed August imitating on the tree outside our apartment building. Alas, the lift-the-leg method would not work in the bathroom. Teaching August to pee like a man was out of my depth. If I had a daughter, I could teach her how to squat and then use her foot to flush toilets in public places. When she grew older, I could advise her on the pros and cons of tampons versus pads, but I had checked *boy* on the adoption placement forms.

Lisa kept telling me, "Let the dishes go. Put your oxygen mask on first." Even though I knew better, I was still suffering under the weight of trying to be a strong Black mother and couldn't shake the disappointment of my latest mom fail, teaching August how to pee standing up. I reluctantly enlisted help from August's godfather and Richard, who had come to visit a few times, even though we never pursued a relationship.

August liked wiggling his hips and watching his little penis jiggle in the hallway mirror, and he had developed a fascination with toilet paper. August would unspool the roll and put as much of it in the toilet as he could before I busted him. Then, he'd wave *bye* like the toilet paper was going on vacation. If I got to the bathroom in time, a stare down would ensue as he eased his little hand over the handle. "Don't do it, August." Of course, he did and as I screeched, "Nooooo" in the garbled slow motion of people falling off buildings in movies, he flushed. Visions of an overflowing toilet bowl, sopping wet copies of *The New Yorker*, rugs floating across the floor, and my two dogs paddling to safety on wet hardwood floors immediately came to mind. Each time, the pipe gods were on my side, and I exhaled with relief.

"Remember Mommy told you to only use three squares? You can stop up the toilet using too much toilet paper." After one too many episodes, I asked, in desperation, "Why didn't you wait for me to wipe your bottom?" Giggling, August, with shorts pulled down, would try to sidestep past me out of the bathroom. He was off to his next caper, having succeeded in giving me a mild heart attack.

After their next *man-time* excursion, an exasperated Rudy reported the young Jedi insisted on sitting to urinate. He said that even after he gave August a bucket to safely stand on, he flat out refused to pee standing. Rudy was flustered and took the failed experiment hard. With a pat on the back, I assured him that he had done his best. I consulted Richard and a couple of other male friends who couldn't exactly remember when they learned to pee standing up, but all agreed August would assume the position when he was ready. I heard what they were saying, but a few months later I asked August if he wanted to try again. I was pressing the issue because I felt inadequate. Other boys his age had achieved that masculine feat and, in my mind, August was behind.

August was a good sport and indulged Operation Pee Standing Up. One day, I decided we just had to face the porcelain god together, August with his Lakers pajama bottoms resting on his slender ankles and me wearing my *let's do this!* face. I commanded him to lift the toilet seat. Momentarily stumped, I didn't know if he was supposed to use one or two hands to hold his penis. Not wanting to break momentum by calling one of the males in his community to ask, I suggested he use two hands. August did not know where to put his hands and neither did I. Was it left over right? Right over left? Did men interlace their fingers underneath their penises and make a circle with their thumbs? My efforts were not working, but August was game. We couldn't stop now. I gambled with left over right and told him to lean his torso forward. After twenty seconds, nothing happened. August gazed up at me with a sheepish grin. I quickly directed him to focus. Trying to trick his bladder into cooperating, I turned the cold water faucet on in the sink. Nothing happened. I suggested using one hand. This seemed a better fit for August, who shoved his fingers in his mouth. With his left hand in position and his stomach distended, we waited. Once again, our mission failed. I had one last trick up my sleeve. Hazyl told me she threw Cheerios into the toilet and told her son to take aim. We had a box atop the fridge. Before I could leave the bathroom, August said, "Mommy, I want to sit down." And he did. When August finally peed standing up, it was a surprise. He did it in his own time, just as the men folk had predicted.

August and Rudy spent lots of man-time together. They would ride around in Rudy's blue Tahoe and spend time at Rudy's parents' home pruning flowers and *fixing* things. Rudy was putty in August's hands. This cantankerous man of a thousand verbal zingers would drive from his home, forty-five minutes away, to watch August and give me a break. We had been friends for close to twenty years, and I couldn't ask for a better godfather for my son. I had always had a lot of male friends and valued their relationship counseling, negotiation strategies when purchasing tires, and help in dealing with male bosses. Becoming a single mother through adoption made me appreciate them even more. I had no shame in asking Rudy or other male friends to talk to August if he was being naughty, play catch with him, or read him a story. Plus, I was tired of fulfilling the cultural expectation that unmarried, single mothers who were gainfully employed were *strong Black women*, defined as not needing or wanting a man.

Because I had a lot of support, most days I did not feel like a single parent, and it probably appeared to the outside world that August and I were satisfied as a duo. The truth, however, was more complicated. I could manage August by myself but felt the sting of my solo status when I was overwhelmed, like the night August escaped from his crib and fell, landing on his head. Or the many nights it took five, maybe ten, tries to get August to remain in his toddler bed. I needed a man, but did not know where I would put him, because my life was consumed with August and work.

As I dipped in and out of the *strong Black woman* section of the bus, my male compadres made it clear they did not trust my judgment regarding four-year-old August. Rudy, Terrance, and Tommy, all childless, felt entitled to say anything they wanted to me about how I was bringing up August. They were quiet when educational choices needed to be made, which was smart since I was the one paying tuition, but they couldn't resist mansplaining why August needed a close-cropped haircut. They spoke with authority on what he should wear (no shorts above the knee), whom he should befriend (boys that would toughen him up), and why he shouldn't carry moo-moo cow outside the house (obviously). Terrance discussed how yoked August's arms were and which sport he would excel in. Rudy decided that August should go to Harvard, and Tommy thought he was soft because he didn't like being tossed in the air. When I corrected August for chewing with his mouth open, Rudy would say, "He's a man." Another time, I fussed at August for not tying his shoelaces, and Tommy said, "Would you get off his head?" All three of them directed me to stop carrying him around. They said he was too big to be carried, but August was still my baby. So what if his spindly legs dangled past my knees?

Their hesitation about my mothering skills were unfounded. August was always neat, clean, and happy. I maintained one or two jobs simultaneously, had lived on my own for years, was pretty level-headed, and let the men in my life do things for me. If only they knew how hard I worked on my damsel-in-distress routine. They expressed that August would be taller and stronger than me by the time he was twelve years old and worried that I would be unable to handle him. They shamed me for being petite and for wearing blue nail polish. In their estimation, I was too feminine to rear a boy by myself. I told them there were thousands of boys in need of a dad in foster care and they could go and adopt one themselves.

Terrance didn't want kids. Rudy had helped raise nephews and great-nieces and great-nephews, and, ironically, hypermasculine Tommy was assisting his sister with her daughter. They meant well, despite their inherent chauvinism. The Y chromosome made the men around me think that because they were men, they were right about everything—and that it was perfectly acceptable to voice their opinions whenever and wherever they felt like it. I tolerated the three amigos because they loved August and they cracked me up with some of their wisdom.

Them: What do you know about raising a Black man in America?

Me: Obviously not as much as you do, but somebody's gotta do it.

Them: Ain't no man gonna marry you now; you got baggage.

Me: Is "M(other)" the new scarlet letter? Tell me.

Them: You didn't want to be pregnant, so that's why you adopted, right?

Me: I never said that.

Them: He's beautiful.

Me: I know. *(swoon)*

Them: A woman can't raise a boy.

Me: Here we go with that nonsense. We do it all the time. Ever hear of a guy named LeBron James?

Them: You didn't want any baby-daddy drama.

Me: What???

Them: He should play ball 'cross town, so he can get some heart and culture and *street smarts*.

Me: I'll give you two out of three.

Them: You can't teach him to pee standing up.

Me: You're right, and when the time comes, you do it.

Them: Mama's boy.

Me: Why, 'cause he's got a mama who loves him and he's a boy?

Them: Men shake hands, not hug.

Me: That's what's wrong with Black men—too scared to be vulnerable.

Them: How are you going to raise a boy without a husband or boyfriend?

Me: You can help until I get one.

Them: You won't ever get married because you and that boy are too close.

Me: So if I neglect him, I'll find a mate tomorrow? Really?!

Them: Boys wear shorts that go past their knees.

Me: Who makes these rules?

Them: He's got a few female traits, but sports will get rid of those.

Me: You came up with that one all by yourself, didn't you?

Them: In twenty years, he'll be callin' us *niggas*.

Me: Just because he's supersmart and attends private school doesn't mean he'll grow up to be Clayton Bigsby.

Them: Get ready for him to bring home a white girl.

Me: As long as he doesn't marry her, it's okay. Just kidding! I will love whomever he loves.

Them: He finally looks urban. Good job.

Me: Fuck you.

Sometimes I argued back, but mostly my responses were *sotto voce*. There was no point in engaging foolishness, bless their misogynistic hearts.

In addition to getting clowned at work, I got mansplained at the barbershop, which was an environment bursting with diverse male energy. At any given hour, a local politician might be sitting in the chair, across from a minister, coach, rapper, executive, or drug dealer. They talked shit to one another about who would whup who in a one-on-one basketball contest, fantasy football brackets, if Pacquiao was ready for Mayweather, sports contracts, politics, and why they did or did not like *Death at a Funeral*. The men at the barbershop laughed loud, held cross conversations, and dapped one another when they entered and exited. Multiple televisions had different sports programs blasting, and the buzz of clippers echoed throughout the building. I had not been to a barbershop since going with an ex-boyfriend in graduate school, but on a recommendation from Lori's husband, I drove August thirty-five minutes to Inglewood twice per month to get a haircut.

I couldn't count the number of times the bromance paused

for a nanosecond when August and I darkened the doorway. The men in there smelled single mother and silently communicated with one another to shut the conversation down. Women who were not barbers or getting haircuts were interlopers. We changed the energy in the room, and men reacted by puffing out their chests, amping up their bravado, or erecting a wall to preserve this sacred space. Respectful of this inner masculine sanctum, I made a point to be as unobtrusive as possible.

I only spoke with the men who made eye contact with me, then buried my head in a magazine or feigned interest in whatever was on the television. August was in heaven, climbing over seats and spinning empty barber chairs. I tried to keep a leash on him, but either the barber or a customer would inevitably say, "He's just being a boy." Or, they would tell August to sit still, and he would, responding to a primal instinct of being the youngest in the pack.

There, I was trying to teach him good manners and respect for other people's property, and they were contradicting me in front of him. But I let my boy be a boy. When it was August's turn, they would ask the type of haircut he would get. Most did what I asked, but every now and then, I got lectured on how I needed to put grease in August's hair and use a boar brush to release his hair's natural oil. One went so far as to tell me to let him take care of August's hair. While he did not add, *'cause you don't know what you're doing*, the implication was in his exasperation with August for crying while he was combing his hair. On another occasion, a barber politely asked if I would step outside. He said, "We can't talk how we want with you in here." He was obviously raised not to curse and act out in front of women, so I did as he asked and waited outside.

After a few months, the drive to Inglewood started getting old. I tried a couple of shops closer to home, but the prices were higher. Nikki cut her son's hair and encouraged me to try it, promising I would save money and time. I set August upon a counter-height dining room chair and wrapped a bath towel around his neck, making sure not to choke him. A comb, brush, oil sheen, clippers, and a bottle of clipper oil were assembled within easy reach on the table. I assumed the role of mommy-barber and combed August's hair out. With *Elmo in Grouchland* cued up on the TV, I powered up the clippers and floundered immediately. I forgot to oil the clippers or use the guard. August jerked when the teeth from the clippers bit his hairline. The sides and top of his hair were uneven, and the back of his head had so many start and stops, it looked like someone popped wheelies on his scalp. I abandoned this adventure without handing him a mirror. August looked like he had a terminal disease. It was too late to have a professional fix it, and we had plans to meet up with school friends. I should have kept him home, but it wasn't his fault his mother had once again stepped out of her lane. I texted my friend a picture in advance, to mitigate the shock and laughter, and back to the barbershop we went.

I made peace with being unable to teach August to pee standing up or be his personal barber. I drew the line at the idea that *men shake hands, not hug.* This caveman advice came from Henry. He was insistent that even a four-year-old boy use this universal male greeting.

It had never occurred to me that there was an expectation for little boys to adhere to a specific masculine salutation. This protocol began early, and there was nothing I could do about it. As August grew older, men reached for his hand upon introduction. Rudy still hugged and kissed him, but Tommy and Terrance introduced the bruh-man handshake to my snaggletoothed boy. Both men were close to or over six feet tall, and August stood waist-high. They announced they would show him the proper way to shake a man's hand and began a tutorial in the office. Tommy practically bent his thick body in half, arced his right hand into the air, gripped August's right hand, and pulled him in close. Having once been a camp counselor, Tommy took a different approach. He would get down on one knee and go through the same motions as Tommy. Usually the handshake ended with August being tickled or unable to withdraw his little hand from theirs. August was proud of his new male skill. It made him one of the boys.

Once we were leaving a playdate with August's friend Michael, and I encouraged August to give Michael's father a handshake and a hug. I added the hug because, after growing up with stoic Henry as a father figure, I believed hugs would have bridged the emotional distance I experienced as a child. Henry was a provider. He did not waste time mollycoddling, though he used congratulatory language like *good job* and a pat on the back to show approval. Ann was definitely the warmer of the two, but women were expected to be affectionate. I was more like Henry and not naturally inclined to more than a wave or warm smile unless I was with a child or someone I was intimate with. Knowing my aversion to being touchy-feely, my best friends would hug and kiss me just to get on my nerves. It would take August's arrival in my life to soften me up. I couldn't get enough of his sweet kisses, and this spilled over to my interactions with adults. I realized I had missed out on growing up with an affectionate male in the house. I would not skip that portion of parenting, believing that nonverbal communication was important to the psychological development of boys.

Positive touch, be it a dap or bruh-man handshake, validated a person's existence. It meant *I see you, I hear you, I love you.* Black boys were criminalized at a young age and needed affection from men to counteract research that discovered that, "Black boys as young as 10 [were] not…viewed in the same light of childhood innocence as their white peers, but [were] instead more likely to be mistaken as older, be perceived as guilty and face police violence if accused of a crime." In this same article, "The Essence of Innocence: Consequences of Dehumanizing Black Children," I read that Black children were perceived to be four-and-a-half times older than white children of the same age. This shortened period of innocence meant less time to spend nurturing warmth and affection, as the focus of parents of Black kids would soon turn to keeping our sons away from gangs, fast women, and drugs.

We would speed up the maturation process believing that if he lived to see eighteen, then twenty-one, and the magic number twenty-five, he would have a chance to live, maybe even have a shot at the American dream.

Before my eyes, as he grew, August was grasping the keys to the man box, the place where he would store his emotions and assume a decidedly male affect. He was picking up masculine gestures and learning the difference between confident eye contact and mean mugging from all the different types of men he had been exposed to. Even if I told August it was okay to cry, he would soon get the message that boys were not supposed to cry, express pain, or share their feelings.

One day at work, I had an infuriating conversation with Terrance, who made a comment out of the blue. "August doesn't have a killer instinct."

"What does that mean?" I looked up from my computer. Terrance's desk was upstairs, but he usually hung out in my office.

He scratched his beard. "He's soft, like a girl."

"Are you serious?"

He was.

"Are you saying this because August is being raised by a single mother?" I asked defensively.

"Yep." He pretended to make a layup against the wall.

"You were raised by your grandmother, and you're not soft."

"True, but I come from the projects. Your son is from Beverly Hills."

"Oh, I see. Because he lives in a nice neighborhood, he's going to get beat up." I pursed my lips.

"Basically."

"Collin, do you hear him?" I called to one of our coworkers. Collin was white, came from the suburbs, and was earning his master's in family therapy.

"White boy Collin knows what up."

Collin damn near turned purple.

"Tell her," Terrance said.

"Yeah, I hate to admit it, but depending on where you live, that could be true."

"For Black men fo' sho'," Terrance added. "Prolly not for white boys."

I shook my head. "That's what's wrong with men. You guys act like if a boy isn't aggressive, he's a punk."

"I'm just sayin'. August has never had a fight or had to fight for anything."

"He's four years old."

"Don't matter." Terrance stood and headed back upstairs.

I yelled after him. "That's dumb. When you have high blood pressure from holding in your emotions, let's see how well having a killer instinct serves you then." I wanted to spare August the anguish of a hypermasculine culture that would protect him on the outside but slowly kill him on the inside, but I could see it was going to be a difficult thing to do.

The myth of Black hypermasculinity even affected parenting

styles, which was why I sent August to private school to avoid the school-to-prison pipeline culture our country had developed. Black mothers attempted to disrupt the inevitable depiction of what it meant to be a man and imposed requirements and strategies to keep our sons safe. From our upbringing, music, movies, breaking news, literature by and about Black men, gossip, and word of mouth, we created a blueprint for raising boys. Because we were not men, there were gaps we did not understand how to fill, so we erred on the side of caution. Some of us either treated our sons like the crown prince, heaping love without discipline, thinking that would keep him close and out of trouble. Or, we unconsciously gave in to hundreds of years of racist social doctrine and overly masculinized our sons, treating them like men when they were still boys. There were negative ramifications for both parenting styles, and the pressure to conform to gender norms was pervasive for dual households and single mothers.

I'm not sure that single mothers had it the hardest. There were many two-parent homes with fathers who worked multiple jobs or who were emotionally absent, and in some ways that seemed even more difficult. Boys living in this dynamic were easy prey to gangs, who offered emotional support and bonding. Humans crave connection with other humans, and when there is a void exacerbated by the effects of institutional racism, Black boys get sucked into a gang's vortex. Black mothers were no match for this undertow.

With a finite window of opportunity available to me, I took

advantage of August's youth to augment his man box with appropriate emotional outlets. In my estimation, a parting greeting with men included a handshake and a hug. That small act of rebellion against our hypermasculine culture was my way of promoting masculine closeness. I also gave him language. August's emotional vocabulary expanded to include the words *frustrated, annoyed, sad, angry, irritated, forgiveness, sorry.*

White people who adopt a Black boy need to know their son will be perceived as hypermasculine. People may fear him or be uncomfortable around him because of their unconscious bias toward Black boys. In school, white female teachers may read his energy as hyper, aggressive, and angry. He may retreat into silence and withhold affection to live up to an image of what it means to be a Black man in America. For those curious about what happens to Black men trapped in their man box, read Michelle Alexander's *The New Jim Crow: Mass Incarceration in the Age of Colorblindness* or listen to Kendrick Lamar or Common, whose beats and lyrics communicate death, quiet desperation, and bitter loneliness. Tupac Shakur wrote a poem, "I Cry," to describe the pain of being unable to openly express sadness, as a judgment of the expectations of Black men in America.

The resonance of society's prejudice didn't just echo in song lyrics, of course. By the time August turned six years old, Ezell Ford, Tamir Rice, Eric Garner, and Trayvon Martin had been murdered by police or a white man. The ongoing disenfranchisement of Black males was well-documented, and widespread homelessness and despair gripped our community throughout the nation. Black parents fought hard to break the cycle of perceived Black hypermasculinity but history, science, cultural judgments, and a laundry list of negative perceptions stood in the way.

Now an observer in the ways of men, I surmised that if more Black men had a chance to just be boys during their child-hoods, our community would be further along, more cohesive, and self-hatred would have less of a foothold. I was determined that August not become one of those shut-down men or become unapproachable to please an archaic ideal of manhood. More than anything, I hoped he would be satisfied with his life and grow into a man who was liked and respected by his peers, the kind of guy who would be invited over for a beer.

Even if I thought parts of the man box were problematic, I under-stood I could not be everything to August. In our case, sports provided the nexus between my helicopter parenting and August's introduction to adult males unrelated to us. In kindergarten, he began playing T-ball in an all-Black baseball league. At first, I attended every practice. Initially, I stayed at the field to watch because we lived too far away to make two trips back and forth, and because the neighborhood the baseball field was located in wasn't the greatest.

My decision to place August in the all-Black league was deliberate. He was five years old and attended a private school that was predominantly white. Black children in those environments needed racial balance. They needed a connection to their people—wealthy, poor, and in between. August needed a village of Black men, not just the ones who were close with our family, and I was grateful to his best friend's mom, Charlie, who invited August to play in the league. On the field with Coach Brookins, Coach Allen, Coach Mike, and other Black men, August got regular adult male attention. The dads took August under their wings and treated him like their own. In addition to learning how to play baseball, they gave him life lessons on conflict resolution, encouraged him to persevere, and made him do push-ups if he wasn't paying attention. August responded positively to these men, and I was happy to not interfere in his male community. By the second season, I dropped August off and went grocery shopping or sat in my car, trusting that the men on the field had our backs.

The other baseball moms and I built a village of Black men and women around our boys that extended beyond sports. We ran an old-school network of loving, disciplining, and supporting them. We bonded over raising Black sons, vegan recipes, politics, microaggressions committed by white female teachers, and our many respective mom fails. A couple of the mothers traveled for work, and we picked up each other's slack with carpool and dinner for the kids. Meanwhile, the dads reached out and invited August to hang with their sons. That not only gave me a much-needed break, but I began to loosen the reins on August. He was becoming an actual person and needed to learn how to be part of a team, how to lead, how to follow, how to recover from mistakes, and how to make decisions for himself. These were spheres where the men folk helped him process every emotion from silliness to frustration to disappointment to anger. I did my best to stay out of the way. August and I had established strong nonfamilial ties with a tight-knit group of like-minded folks, and I was grateful.

Five years into the parenting game, I no longer felt like an imposter on Mother's Day. I gave a simple "Yes, his dad was over six feet" answer to the curious who could see he would grow up to be tall. I grew comfortable explaining he was adopted, and no, I did not know his people. Having a male community was no substitute for a father, of course, but it seemed to take the edge off August's pain. By the time first grade rolled around, Father's Day was no longer a thing. August stopped asking about his biological father, though I checked in with him regularly about his feelings about him. I communicated to August that we could talk about his birth parents any hour of the day, any day of the week, making it clear that his parentage was not a secret nor anything to be ashamed of. I was proud to be in his life and thanked him for choosing me to be his mother. During one of those talks, he advised me that when I got married someday, I would become his second favorite parent. August's desire to have a father had not dissipated, it just shifted from one with blood ties to a man who would love him the way his friends' dads loved them. I was happy with that arrangement, and we shook on my pending demotion.

Though we were secure in our relationship, the irony of being a single mother was that my child would always want a father. There I was in the trenches with him, doing everything I knew to make his life easy, and spending money I did not have to set his trajectory on an upward path, and while August appreciated my sacrifice, he still craved a masculine role model. I chose not to be insulted by his feelings. He spoke his truth, and I rolled with it. My job was to continue to build community and keep positive images of Black men at the forefront of August's life.

Heroes

With my extended community built and one eye trained on August, I turned my attention to our foundation—my family. In September 2012, Henry almost backed off the parking ramp at the Baldwin Hills Crenshaw Plaza. This shook him so much, he let me move his Buick Century. I knew our family was in trouble because normally Henry did not let anyone get behind the wheel of his vehicle. He was still active in church but had the added responsibility of taking care of Ann, who, after caring for her sister Ethel, had herself since been diagnosed with Alzheimer's. Unbeknownst to me, his health was slowly declining. He had been special ordering shoes under the pretense that his feet hurt. My bacon-eating vegetarian grandfather, who ate raw garlic to lower his blood pressure and shopped at Trader Joe's had been gorging on spinach to heal his body. Even after prodding by myself and Helen, Henry kept his health status to himself.

By Thanksgiving, Barack Obama had been reelected, and

Henry's kidneys were shutting down, and his feet had swollen to a size sixteen. I went to his bedside at the hospital. Ann was quiet, seated in a chair near the window.

"Henry, can you hear me?" I stood over him and touched his hair. I had never known how soft it was.

There were no machines in the room, just one tube of oxygen connected to his nose. "Yes, Neffetiti." He never called me Nef. Henry was formal until the day he died.

"Thank you for being a great father and grandfather." My voice caught. "I learned so much from you."

"Okay, okay, okay. You're welcome." Henry went on to tell me he wanted yellow cake and a big party. His voice was higher and happier for this normally stoic man. Henry was borderline cheerful as he described the dessert he wanted and telling me who to invite to the party. I couldn't believe it; he was planning his repast. I settled in and kept asking what he wanted and who should attend the party until Ann signaled she was ready to go home.

"Henry, I love you."

"Yes, yes." He nodded and smiled.

Two days later, he was gone. At eighty-seven years old, Henry Lee Hawthorne Jr. died of renal failure/malnutrition/bone cancer in December 2012. That morning, I waited for Ann to finish breakfast and broke the sad news. She quietly cried and covered her face. I had only seen Ann cry two other times. She had been a pillar of strength my entire life, and it was my turn to hug her and say, "It's all right."

It's strange how life works. I named my son for an esteemed playwright but could have easily named him Henry Lee. August was so much like his great-grandfather, it wasn't even funny. He possessed the same erudition, love of books, and analytical mind. In a way, it felt like Henry was still with me. I could already see what a gentleman August was going to become.

Of course, Henry had preplanned all the details of his funeral. He left instructions regarding his obituary, burial outfit, number of flowers, and what would happen at the cemetery. Henry wanted to be buried in a smoking jacket and pajama bottoms, noting that it was ridiculous to spend money on a suit no one would see. Unable to find his smoking jacket from the 1960s, we settled on a velvet robe. We gave Henry the send-off he requested and his half brother officiated the service. August and my nieces were enthralled by the twenty-one-gun salute for the proud veteran of the United States Navy. We all watched as his casket was placed in the mausoleum.

Henry lived a good life. He was generous and kind to people. I was honored to be his daughter and deeply thankful that some part of his spirit would live on through my son.

August Gets His Wish

Something was in the air in 2013. First grader August and I were a dynamic duo, he, the intellectually curious young Jedi, and I, half-Tiger, half-Western mom. In January, I added certified PS-MAPP trainer to my long resume. Instead of waiting to be invited to speak as a guest at trainings for prospective foster/adoptive parents, I would be part of the trio that led them. I was writing about Black people and adoption for free on my blog and other websites and applying for fellowships and scholarships for artist parents. I had work-life balance, and I felt it was time to fully resume my previous career aspirations as a well-paid full-time writer. Little did I know that my carefully crafted house of cards would be hijacked by a baby girl.

While I had privately flirted with the idea of a second child, I had no real intentions of raising two kids as a single parent. Confident that adding to my brood was fiscally not a good idea, I ignored August when he began asking for a little sister. After all, we had two dogs and a betta fish named Quinn Brandon. Our lives were filled to the brim with school, traveling, sports, two jobs, and writing about adoption and Black motherhood. How could I afford tuition, childcare, and one more mouth to feed? The biggest question was where would a new baby sleep? August's room was overgrown with trains, race cars, and dinosaurs. Meanwhile, my room hosted unopened boxes, bare walls, and stuff under the bed. We had outgrown our two-bedroom apartment before even moving in, and until Mommy's war chest overflowed, that was where we would be living. I was still single, running back and forth from my apartment to Ann's house to check in on her as much as I could. And I was spending some time on the phone apologizing to friends who had become moms before me. I used to speak out of turn advising them to add another activity to their already hectic schedules.

I started with Lisa. "Hey, girl. Remember that time I suggested you guys join Jack and Jill so Derek and Alicia could be part of its Black youth leadership program?"

"Yeah."

"I was wrong. I'm sorry. My life is bananas with one child, and I can see how one more activity can upset the applecart."

"I wasn't studyin' you." She giggled. "You'd figure it out sooner or later."

After Lisa, I went through my contact list making amends, and contemplating an old feeling. The mommie-jones was back. Once again, my antennae for all things baby went up.

I began entertaining the thought of a second child because

August had badgered me into submission. He said he needed somebody to play with. More specifically, he wanted a baby. He didn't understand that another baby for a single woman was financially counterintuitive. August would not be doing the heavy lifting and had no clue about the physical logistics of juggling baby gear, his bat bag, and backpack. What would I do when one kid was sick and the other was bouncing off the walls? Who would help me? Why would I upset our lives when August could make his bed, tie his shoes, get his own snack, speak clearly, and entertain himself? By all accounts, we were winning. I had already given back to society and didn't owe anybody anything. But August didn't care about any of that; he wanted a sister.

I ignored his request for months and then had a revelation. August had such a big heart. He'd make a great big brother and deserved to have a sibling. He already had my undivided attention, attended private school, had trophies from four sports, and was spoiled by family and friends. The downside of life with just mom was that he could grow up to be selfish, thinking the world revolved around him and that everyone loved him the way I did. All of that indulgence amounted to the risk of him becoming like the entitled douchebags who enrolled in my college history course and demanded extra credit because they forgot to take the midterm exam. I didn't want that for him.

The other truth was that additions to a family were about the parents. It was our desire to be needed and our love of growing a little person into a full-fledged adult that often motivated having multiple children. Being a mother, though nerve-wracking at times, was a huge slice of heaven. I could not imagine my life without my precious gift of a son. On the other hand, single motherhood was no walk in the park. Even so, on the eve of paying for summer camp, purchasing the next size up of baseball cleats, and saying goodbye to kindergarten, I grudgingly admitted that I had the sweetest hangover from parenting a little one.

Still, I tried to talk myself down. In public, I nodded in agreement with other parents of only children about the emotional and financial stress multiple children brought. I did the math and, sure enough, the numbers would not stretch to cover two kids. But then I remembered the other numbers. Those that represented the hundreds of thousands of children in foster care. They needed permanent homes. Had I not adopted August, I shudder to think of what would have happened to him. Would he have become one of those boys selling candy in grocery store parking lots? He could have languished in foster care or he could have been placed in another healthy, stable home. Who knew?

I tried to resist the self-guilt trip I was on and set about to break August's heart with an offer to buy a puppy, when a random conversation during jury duty changed everything. An older married Black woman, Linda, and I were waiting in front of the courtroom after lunch. We exchanged pleasantries, and she asked if I had any children. I told her about August and shared that he was adopted. Linda got really excited and asked if I knew his people. Nonplussed by my revelation that I had adopted a stranger, she told me about her nineteen-year-old son, who was a sophomore in college. He was doing well and would be returning to Berkeley in two weeks. I listened politely, and when she finished, I asked if they had other children. "No," she said, admitting she and her husband thought they could not afford two kids. "We made a mistake. We would have had to work a little harder, but we would have been okay." She regretted playing it safe. I went home that day and took a deep breath.

Speaking with Linda made me proud that I had not let fear keep me from becoming a mother through adoption. The decision was made: I would find a sibling for August. I emotionally prepared for what awaited me: social workers, visits with the birth mom, people telling me how good I looked to have two kids, the same people telling me I was nuts for adopting two kids by myself. I knew there was no way I could bear to look back over my life and feel sadness for choosing practicality over one more mouth to feed. I would draw from the resolve of Black women and mothers who came before me and help another child. I would make it work. I decided to begin the adoption process…again.

In February 2013, I was hired to co-lead a class with community college representative Mirza Gonzalez and Jordy Hayes, CSW (clinical social worker). My life as an adoptive parent had come full circle. I went from being a prospective foster/adoptive parent to speaker at PS-MAPP classes to trainer. I was in my element. Once I gave in to adopting another child, I attended an orientation sponsored by DCFS. I learned that because I was a certified PS-MAPP trainer, it would be a conflict of interest for me to adopt through DCFS. If I wanted to foster or adopt, I would have to sign up with a foster family agency (FFA). An FFA was a private entity run by a licensed social worker who contracted with DCFS. They offered a curriculum very similar to PS-MAPP and the pool of children from foster care was the same. The biggest difference was cost and demographics. Some of the FFAs catered to the LGBTQ community and others were race-specific to attract more Latinxs or Samoans to foster care and adoption. Once again, Lori directed me to an agency run by her former coworker. I completed classes in April. The home study would follow, along with the foster/adoption match paperwork.

In the meantime, Donna invited me to speak at her PS-MAPP class on April 9, 2013. I gave my usual spiel, going through my whole journey with the system and making note of the fact that August would just have to be mad about not having a relationship with his biological siblings until he got older. During the break, Donna and I spoke about making a connection with August's siblings.

"I know your adoption is closed, but you might consider speaking to the adoptive mother of August's younger brother, Isaac. Mrs. Carson is very nice. She's like Mrs. Wilson."

"I tried that already with Ms. Smith."

"Ah, Ms. Smith." Donna shook her head. "This is different. Mrs. Carson is sane. Also, August could benefit from meeting some family. It won't hurt."

"I'll think about it."

"I'll even facilitate a visit."

The only reason I even entertained August meeting another sibling was because I respected Donna and trusted her judgment. And I had to admit that while I loved having August all to myself, I should not stand in the way of his chance to have a relationship with his brother. Damn. August's adoption had been final for four years, and there was still fallout.

Mrs. Carson and I spoke on the phone a couple of times. By then, I learned that August had an additional sister, Shay. We traded Renata stories and agreed that she had produced very smart children, and it was too bad she had not gotten herself together. Mrs. Carson invited us to Isaac's birthday party. Several weeks later, Donna, Kisha, August, and I attended a birthday party for Isaac at his home.

The party was in full swing and children were everywhere. There were at least thirty kids laughing, spinning, and jumping, and almost all of them were foster children. Isaac's adoptive mother had a cadre of Black foster mom friends who gathered their foster kids, of all races, together frequently. They felt it was important the kids knew they were not the only ones living in out-of-home care. That was awesome. August did not have that type of support. The only adopted kids we knew were born overseas and had white parents. Those transracial adoptees were never foster children, and their parents had no clue how the public foster care system worked.

We were welcomed with open arms, and August was

introduced as Isaac's brother. The boys hugged each other and scampered off to play. Mrs. Carson, Isaac's adoptive mom, pointed out August and Isaac's little sisters, Shay and Anaya, and Leatha, Shay's godmother. I was openly surprised that there was yet another baby. Donna didn't know about Anaya either. I asked Mrs. Carson if I could hold her. That was my first mistake. Anaya, who was six months old, looked just like me, and Kisha leaned over and said, "That's your baby." I ignored her. Anaya was cute, but I didn't know what to do with a little girl. I had a good handle on raising a boy and wasn't ready for a new learning curve. But Kisha and all of my friends who saw Anaya's picture said the same thing, "That's your baby."

Mrs. Carson was in the process of adopting two-year-old Shay and planned to adopt Anaya at a later time. I congratulated her and shared that I had begun the process to be recertified to adopt. We had a great time. Not only did August leave that visit with a brother and two sisters, I returned home wondering what it would be like to mother the baby girl I held in my arms. Her essence lingered, and several weeks later, I could still feel her tight grasp on my finger. Whenever I scrolled through the photos we took that day, my eyes lingered on the picture Kisha snapped of us. Our resemblance was uncanny. We shared the same coloring, brown eyes, and tiny curly Afros. We looked like twins separated by a few decades. I couldn't shake the feeling that this little girl belonged with me.

The leaves on August's family tree were slowly filling up. I

couldn't be happier for him and agreed to facilitate his relationship with Isaac, Shay, and Anaya. Mrs. Carson and I spoke on
the telephone and so did the boys. They hit it off right away, and
we went back to their home on a third occasion for a playdate.
Shay spent a lot of time on glamorous outings with Leatha, so we
didn't spend as much time with her. She was all bows and painted
nails. I remember thinking that I could never keep up with that.
It was unfortunate that Renata's life was so off the rails, but at
least the kids would not have to deal with a biological mother who
muddied the waters by being in and out of their lives.

Mrs. Carson and her posse of foster mothers were *sheroes*.
Those single Black mothers were not Black welfare queens. They
were generous citizens, called to help children in need. Most
participated in adoption ministries sponsored by their respective churches. Others were brought into foster/adoption care by
friends. Those ladies were kind and loving to the kids in their midst
and those with whom they had no connection. They honored the
children's biological parents and actively worked to reunite families
broken by drugs, abuse, incarceration, mental health issues, and
neglect. They were not rich, nor trying to prosper off the small
stipends offered by the County. They were invisible Black women
at the margins of motherhood—just some of thousands of unseen
women across the country making the same sacrifices and quietly
changing the lives of the children they mothered.

Just over one month later, the foster family agency approved
and certified my home study for an infant. I told my family that

I was adopting again. This time Ann laughed. She said, "You obviously know what you're doing," and kept laughing.

My cousin Ray immediately suggested that I'd want one child of each gender. I argued him down. "For starters, girls are more expensive than boys. Let's take clothes. Boys need a shirt, a pair of pants, shorts if you live in Los Angeles, clean tennis shoes, and toys. Girls have to be accessorized. They needed matching socks, hair bands, earrings, sandals, tennis shoes, boots, and Mary Janes in suede and patent leather." And while I had those things in my own closet, it never crossed my mind to make those purchases in miniature.

Meanwhile, I was happy with my son, and while August had asked for a sister, adopting another boy seemed like a no-brainer. I had a male community, which Ray was part of, and knew they would shepherd another young brother along. My son's hand-me-down toys and clothes were washed and waiting. Plus, I already had a daughter, my dog Sunday, who was twelve years old and in possession of more attitude than the law allowed.

I decided to stick with what I knew and roll another boy child out to the promised land. I talked all that smack but secretly thought of Anaya often. I hated to admit it, but she had crawled into my spirit. She was an angel in a blue dress and, over time, the idea of having a daughter became less far-fetched. All my excuses for not wanting a girl child to mold and raise in my image went out the window. Anaya was spoken for, but maybe, just maybe, I'd surprise August with the sister he had been begging for.

All my plans went on hold one day when Tamala, one of August's nine previous social workers, called. Due to a health emergency, Anaya and Shay needed a new placement. Since August was their sibling, she asked if I would take them. Tamala stated that the sisters had to remain together. I totally understood and agreed that was the best course of action. The girls and Isaac had been together since birth, and there was no point in separating them, even if August was also their brother. I explained the physical limitations of my apartment and that I had only been certified for an infant. Tamala said I could get an exception so that Shay and August could share a room, and Anaya would stay with me in a crib. I knew that emotionally and financially, three children would kill me. I declined. I promised to visit the girls in the next foster home.

A few days later, August and I left town. Tricia, one of my best friends from college, had been diagnosed with leukemia, and we took a road trip to spend time with her. When we returned, I learned there was a slim chance that Anaya and Shay would be separated. Shay would live with her godmother, Leatha, and Anaya would come with us. Once again, my friends rallied and I was given a crib, clothing, bottles, and toys. There was no hiding these items from August. Instead of getting his hopes up about Anaya's placement with us, I told him we were getting a baby but didn't know who it was. It wasn't a complete lie. In the foster system, girls often found placements faster than boys. Shay and Anaya were young, cute, and biological siblings—lots of people would want to scoop them up. That was too much to explain to August, so I gave him the CliffsNotes version of foster care and adoption and told him to be patient.

I was still in contact with Mrs. Carson, and August and I attended one of the sibling visits with Isaac and the girls at a neutral location. Instead of a joyous reunion, the air was heavy with misery. Isaac was sad and crying. He wanted his sisters and his life to return to normal. August was confused, and Mrs. Carson was angry that a minor health challenge opened the floodgates for the girls to be placed outside her home. The foster family agency she was working with assured her that they would be returned, but once the court got involved, the judge determined that Shay and Anaya would be better off in a different environment. I was caught in the middle. Happy for August to spend time with his family and glum at how quickly everyone's life was turned upside down. Before leaving, we promised to see them again.

The whole situation was beyond all of our control. I wanted what was best for the girls and for August. While Mrs. Carson and Isaac had a relationship with Renata and the older brothers, August had no one. He had not seen his older siblings since his first birthday. That chapter had been closed for nearly seven years, and suddenly, a lifeline was thrown his way. Tamala was the intermediary between us and the girls' attorney. The County was insistent the sisters stay together, and I concurred. Mrs. Carson and I developed a friendship during this period. I mostly listened as she shared how devastated they were about the turn of events.

There was nothing we could do but trust the process and wait to learn what the judge at Children's Court decided.

About six weeks later, Tamala called. Through a series of events that only Mrs. Carson could speak to, the judge officially decided that Shay would go with Leatha and Anaya would live with us. Really? I remember clutching my cell phone, knowing this turn of events to be the work of a divine intervention. The call was bittersweet, though. Our gain was Mrs. Carson and Isaac's loss. With the stroke of a pen, August had the sister he always wanted. Anaya shared half of August's DNA and in her, he had a small piece of his biological mother. I told August the news before he went to bed that night. Unable to sleep, my six-year-old immediately began making plans of all of the things he would teach his ten-month-old sister.

On October 12, 2013, August and I began our regular routine. We walked the dogs, ate breakfast, and headed off to Saturday science class. Baseball practice would follow, though we had to make a pit stop first. Anaya, Shay, Leatha, and Tamala would be waiting for us at Mrs. Nichols's, the current foster mother's home. I was nervous. The emotional roller coaster we had been on finally reached its conclusion. Once we picked Anaya up, there was no turning back. When August's class ended, we jammed over to Mrs. Nichols's house. Everybody was waiting for us. As I signed the foster care placement papers, Tamala informed me that Anaya had developmental delays. While she could sit up and hold her own bottle, she had not tried to crawl and made sounds like a younger baby, not like a child getting ready to speak. She would need a lot of attention and nurturing to get her on track. None of that scared me. I had solid mom legs underneath me now, and a village of support. I was up for the challenge this time.

Since beginning my journey to adoption, I had grown significantly as a mother. Smarter and wiser, I had hands-on experience, knew how to access resources, and could love a child I did not birth. Labels did not faze or scare me. Anaya would receive the best care and the same advantages August had. Despite my early misgivings, I was ready to mother a daughter. I still believed that Black baby boys needed rescuing from the foster care system, but it was time to answer the call for a little sista. Her arrival on October 12 was already a seminal date in my family. It was Ann's birthday, and in 2013, she turned eighty-eight. Anaya's arrival felt like the passing of the torch.

August ended up skipping baseball practice that day, opting to show Anaya off to Ann, my mother, and Helen. We took her home, and August wanted to do everything for her. He helped change her diapers, fed her, and held her bottle while she drank. He read to her and kept the dogs a safe distance away. August was protective of his baby, and their chemistry was obvious. He was smiling so hard, the dimples in both cheeks made an appearance. While Anaya napped, he drew a picture. In the history of the world, there had never been a sun so yellow, grass so green, or an ocean so blue. Anaya was the cherry on top of his sundae. Before he went to bed that night, he said that getting his sister was the best day in the universe. I stared at my sleeping baby. August was right; this was the best day. Anaya was beautiful and the perfect addition to our family. Now she needed a new name to signify her new start. I chose Cherish, knowing that we would love this child to the moon and back.

A week later, Cherish and I went to see Dr. Dolan. I gave her Cherish's medical history and Tamala's prediction that due to prematurity and a difficult birth, she might have every delay in the book. Dr. Dolan finished her examination and asked if I thought anything was wrong with Cherish. "I'm not a doctor and have only been a mother for six years, but she seems fine to me."

Dr. Dolan agreed. "There's nothing wrong with her. She is a little behind on waving and smiling. Parents forget those are learned behaviors and babies need to see examples of other people doing them. As for her gastric reflux, give her solids."

When August returned home from school, I enlisted his help in catching Cherish up on developmental milestones. He took his job seriously, and at her next checkup, Cherish, who had been underweight, was plump and on schedule. My daughter easily blossomed into the sweetest little terror God ever made. From the moment she came home, she acted like she knew us. Our resemblance was uncanny, and I suspected that she and August had planned her arrival well before we met. There were too many coincidences for our deep connection to be anything other than divine.

Despite my joy at watching August and Cherish bond, caring for two children threw me into a tailspin. I was exhausted, juggling social workers, keeping up with August's busy schedule, and taking the kids to see Mrs. Carson and Isaac on a regular basis. We did not want to lose that connection. Nancy watched Cherish at her day care for two months before retiring and moving more than an hour away, and I had to find a new childcare situation. Rudy was super helpful and so was my mother, who was now living in Los Angeles to care for Ann, whose Alzheimer's had advanced. August's classmates' parents, a rainbow coalition of white, Black, and Asian mothers, surprised me with a $400 Target gift card and welcomed Cherish into our tight-knit community.

I loved having a daughter. She helped me hit my stride as a woman and as a mother. Apparently, I needed her as much as she needed me. Cherish would help me find my way back to myself. I was no different from any other mother who got lost in the parenting shuffle. I did not want to go back down the road of being a frumpy, harried mother, but that's who I was for the first two years of her life. I had to make a concerted effort to model self-care to my daughter by getting pedicures, reading a book, or going out with the friends who hung in there with me, as I emotionally, physically, and financially adjusted to having two children. I had committed to my new normal and had to set a good example of what it meant to be a Black woman in America. Black girl magic was fine but more importantly, Cherish would not get tripped by the strong Black woman archetype. I would teach her that there was strength in asking for help, and that everybody needs somebody.

Because August had a male community, so did Cherish. I shuffled the deck a little when a few of the guys moved away, but she was surrounded by men who understood that girls need men in their lives too. Cherish even inspired some of my hesitant family members to step forward after hanging back for years. Helen was first to raise the white flag. One day she confessed, "You sure showed us. Your kids are happy, and you are a great mom." I was vindicated.

August and Cherish had distinct personalities, and I had to step my parenting game up. August was more introspective, while Cherish was likely to be standing on top of the table ready to jump. I had to remain one step ahead of her, careful not to squelch her zest for life while encouraging her to use her powers for good. It was evident that Cherish was a boss from day one.

Knowing I had such a strong-willed child raised my racial and gender antennae even higher. Her intersectional experience would be similar to mine, except her exposure to positive images of Black girls and Black women would happen sooner. It was imperative that she saw herself as we saw her: sweet, loved, and wanted.

Too many Black girls dabbled in self-hatred due to a lack of Black female protagonists in literature, television shows, and movies. Cherish needed to know that Black was beautiful and she was enough. That lesson started at home with a toy chest of dolls. She had a diverse collection of sizes and shapes but the majority of the dolls were Black with brown skin, brown eyes, and curly hair.

222 | NEFERTITI AUSTIN

I regularly complimented her textured, thick hair and her ability to think on her feet. While August had to study a problem like the best way to clean dog pee off the floor, Cherish was already reaching for a paper towel. I took her and August to see *Hidden Figures* and for months, she kept asking about the ladies and the rocket. *Doc McStuffins* and *Dora the Explorer* were on heavy rotation in our home, and I finally found one adoption book written by a Black female adoptee who was adopted by Black parents. *Heart Picked: Elizabeth's Adoption Tale* by Sara Crutcher was a cute story written for older adoptees.

Thirteen months after first meeting Cherish, we waited in the courthouse to finalize her adoption. She was adorable in a black, white, and gray chevron-patterned dress with sequins, black tights, and black patent leather Mary Janes. Her little ears were pierced, and her hair was in three puff balls. August wore his best winter sweater and khakis, and I sported a sleeveless black dress and hot pink arm cuff from Ghana.

This was my absolute last adoption, and I wanted all of us to experience National Adoption Day on Saturday, November 22, 2014. August was old enough to understand that his sister would join us as part of our forever family, and I wanted him to witness all the pomp and circumstance. The courthouse was a circus of children, parents, social workers, and lawyers. Music played, cookies and punch were available, and local news stations were interviewing teens and adoptive parents. Multicolored balloons softly bobbed against the ceiling. The festive atmosphere was contagious, and there were so many happy people in the building. As a mother for the second time, I had developed compassion for my mother and was happy she joined August, Lori, Tricia, Kisha, my good friend Laurie, and me at the ceremony. Judge Redmond was not available, so Judge Marshall presided over our adoption. The outcome was the same, Cherish Danielle Austin was now and forever a member of the Austin family.

Cherish's adoption closed that chapter in my life, and I was doubly blessed. If I wasn't so religiously ambivalent, I'd go to church and testify about the miracle of our family made through adoption.

Boy Child in the Promised Land

Mothering two children was exhilarating and required me to add a *Mother of Black Girls* hat to the fifteen others I currently wore. I lost a few friends because there was little time to do anything other than work and manage my family. I would get a social life one day. In the meantime, all of my energy went to my kiddos and at last, the mommie-jones was satisfied. I might look like a single mother with two children trailing after me, but I would walk through fire for these children, and it was my choice every step of the way.

With a historian for a mama, August knew he shared a birthday with Dr. Martin Luther King Jr. This gave him gravitas among his peers. He took having a Black man in the White House for granted, because President Barack Obama was the first president's name he learned. It wasn't until first grade that August memorized the names of the previous forty-three presidents and noticed they were all white men. I felt responsible to teach him about slavery and how his great-grandparents sat in the back of the bus until they moved west. We discussed segregation and how times had changed, but that Black boys still had a rough time in America. It broke my heart to tell August that no one would look at him and assume he was a train aficionado or catcher for the championship Cardinals. The opposite would be true. White people would see a Black boy and judge him according to their preconceived notions.

August might be stereotyped as loud, violent, and not-as-good-as white boys his age. When he misbehaved at school or in public, the negative consequences were greater for him than for his white classmates. I had a firsthand experience with this happening when August was labeled disruptive for shouting out an answer in class. This happened a couple of times and during parent-teacher conferences, I explained that while August should raise his hand, I would not dampen his enthusiasm for learning. He loved school and sometimes overflowed with information. When I asked August what was going on, he said, "I did raise my hand, but she wouldn't call on me." From his perspective, the solution was to say the answer while his hand was in the air.

August did not understand unconscious bias or that when Peter, who was white, shouted out an answer, he was described as *eager*. His white teachers could relate to Peter because he reminded him of their brothers or fathers. August did not. He was the tallest in the class, known to be very bright, with a big voice and matching laugh. The very things that made him who he was got him into trouble from kindergarten through fourth grade. Even after more parent-teacher conferences, I had to remind August that though he spent the majority of his time with mostly white children and white adults, some of whom loved him, he might be treated differently because of the color of his skin. I counseled him about how quickly he would be judged, and unless he was on the basketball court, not to give white people an excuse to call him *aggressive*. We already struggled with teachers calling him *angry*, when he may have been frustrated or annoyed or irritated by his classmates. Confused that he was not the apple of everyone's eye, August wanted to know why.

"You are not white. You cannot do what they do," I explained. To his school's credit, the administration took the complaints of Black parents to heart and made significant changes in the language used to describe boys' behavior. They got on board with educating faculty about microaggressions and their own unconscious biases and incorporated more inclusive images and narratives in the curriculum. I wished all institutions were as open to change as his school was, and I thanked the head of school, former director of admission, and assistant heads of school for attempting to be woke.

As a mother of Black children, I was often the bearer of bad news about how my kid would be perceived in the world. This was one of many burdens parents today carry trying to raise school-aged children of color in a racist climate. We instructed our boys and girls to be good citizens and a credit to the human race. We taught them to avoid being a stereotype threat. They did not have to be who white people thought they were. Just because *they* thought all tall Black boys had hoop dreams or Black people with hard-to-pronounce names were unqualified applicants or that single Black mothers were Black welfare queens did not make it so. Their lives depended on us being honest and equipping them with age-appropriate tools to ensure their physical and emotional safety. On trips to the grocery store when he was younger, I admonished August, "Keep your hands to yourself."

"Why, Mama?"

"So that no one accuses you of stealing." I squeezed his hand tightly.

"What's stealing?"

"Taking something that doesn't belong to you."

"Like that time you ate my Halloween candy without asking?"

I laughed. "Yes. But seriously, sometimes white people think Black boys are bad, even when you aren't doing anything. Let's not give anyone in this store or any other place a reason to bother us."

"Okay, Mama." August thought for a moment. "Does this mean I can't go to the toy aisle?"

I took a deep breath. I was asking a lot of him, but the sooner he learned how he would be perceived by white people, the better. "Um…yes, but the rule is…"

"I know. I know. Don't touch anything."

"And don't talk to strangers."

At home we role-played how to handle himself if he was ever stopped by the police. "August, make eye contact. Respond 'yes, sir' and 'no, sir.'"

I grew tired of seeing my Black sisters crying on the news over the loss of their babies, our babies. No matter our zip code or where we spent vacations, our kids needed to know where they were and to act accordingly. Life was patently unfair, and I prayed that things would be different for August's kids someday.

Being a Black parent was nerve-wracking and scary at times. Danger seemed to lurk around every corner, and yet I had to appear calm and in charge. My children would be programmed to thrive and simultaneously be on the lookout for booby traps with repercussions disproportionately higher for kids of color: lack of access to high-paying careers, sexism, racism, gangs, mental illness, drugs, incarceration, and premature death at the hands of law enforcement. August, and now Cherish, would learn how to code switch, which would be their most powerful survival mechanism. Black children had to gain the ability to assess their audience and surroundings. I had already begun this process with August, and as Cherish grew older, she would learn how to carry herself with class and dress age appropriately (and that was not always enough), because Black girls were overly sexualized at a young age and vulnerable to rape and human trafficking. Knowing that microaggressions were not just reserved for Black boys, she would learn to express herself, so as not to be accused of having an attitude or being an angry Black woman for simply rolling her eyes. However, if the occasion called for it, Cherish would have permission to use all of her words to defend herself. I would preempt an assault on her self-esteem with dolls and protagonists who looked like her, so she could take pride in her brown skin, kinky curly hair, and dark brown eyes. And if she ever asked why it seemed that only blond-haired, blue-eyed girls got to be on commercials and on the cover of kids' books, I would explain that it was racism and another attempt at her erasure.

My kids were young and had all of the time in the world; except they didn't have all of the time in the world. August was a Black boy, assumed to be less innocent than he was, and Cherish was a Black girl, thought to be less beautiful, less smart, less kind, less everything. I didn't want to talk about race every day, every week, or even every month, but the political animus against August's hero, President Obama, was escalating. First Trayvon Martin, then Tamir Rice, Ezell Ford, Eric Garner, Freddie Gray, and so many other Black boys and men died. Then Sandra Bland, one of fifteen unarmed Black women killed by police, died in a jail cell. I had to keep my sleeves rolled up.

Cherish was still a toddler who drank warm milk, but August was ten years old and nervous about the new president. His consciousness was raised and he feared that the bully in the White House would come for him the way he came for undocumented immigrants and people from Muslim countries. I found myself easing his uncertainty and reassuring him we would get through this. Black people had weathered worse.

Bad Mama Jamas

With a fourth grader and three-year-old, I had less time than ever. Henry had gone to glory, and Ann could no longer live alone. Alzheimer's disease was wreaking hell on all of us and turned my rational, sweet grandmother into a firecracker. We tried hiring caregivers, but Ann didn't want just anybody in her house. She wanted to water the lawn and her roses herself. She insisted on frying bacon and cleaning the stove, flames ablaze, in her bathrobe. My mother became her primary caregiver.

When Diane first arrived back in California, I made an effort to spend time with her. My kids and I lived about five minutes away and visited with her often. Our reunion was tepid. Too much time had passed. Not enough words had been spoken. We would never be mother and daughter in the traditional sense, and I was okay with that. I had hoped that time had matured her and she would be a grandmother extraordinaire. But while she babysat from time to time and took the kids to the movies, she mostly did things for herself like shop, listen to CDs, buy bootleg DVDs, and watch television. She was diabetic, walked with a limp, and had gained a considerable amount of weight. Years of drug addiction had exacted their revenge.

My mom wanted Ann to sit and rest, but my strong-willed grandmother wasn't having it. Ann had worn Diane out, and my mother returned to Houston one year later. That was the most time I'd spent with her since I was eight years old, and her departure was uneventful. I was happy that my nieces and kids got to spend time with her and grateful for the lesson I learned that year: Diane was who she was, and she wasn't about to change now.

March of the following year dealt our family a huge blow. My mother was diagnosed with a rare form of cervical cancer. The odds of survival were slim and she was given eleven months to four years to live. I told August right away.

"Grammy is very sick," I told him.

"What's wrong with her?"

"She has cancer. It's pretty aggressive, and she might die."

August was in the fifth grade, and Cherish was four years old. He liked when Grammy came to town. "Like Grandpa Henry?"

"Yes." I hugged him.

"I will miss her," he said softly and cried.

Irony of all ironies, Diane's oncologist's first name was Nefertiti. I got her cell phone number and called her every two weeks. Because I stayed on top of my mom's prognosis, I knew that my mother was lying about her medical status to avoid some of the treatment for her cancer.

"I'm afraid to have a hysterectomy," she told me. She kept missing appointments to delay the surgery, making excuses each time.

Fed up, I finally told her, "Surgery is your choice, and if you don't want to have it, don't have it. But don't lie. Don't play games."

She got the hysterectomy.

Cancer united my mother, brother, Helen, and I. We agreed not to tell Ann, who we had moved to a memory care unit at a senior living facility. We spent lots of time on the phone with each other, sharing what new information we received from Diane's oncologist. Helen worried that the pain meds mixed with methadone were not good for her. I alternated between being pissed at her for lying about what the doctor said and showing compassion for a woman who did not seem to understand or care that lying delayed treatment. Diane was proud of how only one in a thousand people had the type of cancer she had. It became a badge of honor. When it became apparent she did not grasp the severity of her situation, I took over communication with the oncologist, surgeon, nurse, and medical insurance workers. It was a lot to navigate, and I knew she couldn't do it. Without the assistance of my cousin Kisha, who was a licensed clinical medical social worker, not even I would have known the right questions to ask or what to do with the information I received.

In July, Kareem went to Houston and stayed with Diane for

three weeks. He drove her to chemotherapy treatments and kept Helen and I up-to-date on her health. I suspected that was a healing trip for mother and son, whose relationship swung from a close affection to screaming obscenities at each other. He had always missed his mother and needed her in a way I did not. I stayed home. Work and lack of childcare was my excuse. The truth was, I did not want to go. I wasn't ready.

My mom went into a brief remission in August. She declared during that phase that she would not endure treatment again. The nausea was painful, and her whole body hurt. At the first of the year, her screens revealed the cancer had returned with a vengeance. It was in her pancreas.

On a conference call with Helen, Kareem, and myself, Diane said, "I'm not afraid to die."

"Mom, I love you. All is forgiven."

Kareem said, "Thanks, Mom. Now you are free; you don't have to worry about anything anymore." When we hung up, I booked a flight to Houston.

————————

There was no one to meet me at the airport when I arrived, and I drove straight to the hospice center. It was shortly after midnight, and my mother was asleep. I called her name, and she opened unfocused eyes. It took her a minute, but she shrieked, "Nef, I'm so happy you're here." I held her hand and she kept saying, "I love you. I love you so much."

"I love you too."

Her hospital room was large and the television was on in the background. She looked comfortable and six months pregnant. The tumor was spreading from her pancreas to her stomach, with no end in sight. Her legs and arms were smooth, and she was smiling, at peace. There wasn't much to say, so I played one of her favorite songs on my iPhone. George Michael's "Careless Whisper" flooded the room. She tapped her fingers and hummed along. "Music was something we always had in common," she said dreamily.

"Kareem and Helen are coming. Promise you won't die before they get here."

"I promise." She smiled.

The next day, I picked Kareem and Helen up from the airport. I caught them up on my visit and drove them directly to the hospice center. We spent most of the day with her, her brother Eldridge, and her husband, Marcus. Though she slept on and off, she knew we were there with her. The doctor informed us there was nothing to be done and it was best to move her to a different hospice. We spent the better part of the day visiting the new place, and then I completed the intake paperwork on my mother's behalf. While Helen made plans to remain with her sister until she transitioned, Kareem stayed one week, and I left after four days. There was nothing more to be done.

Five days after returning home, the call came. My mother had died. I went back to Houston two days later. I needed to be in her space. I needed to know her underneath the drugs, parental neglect, and the rut she got stuck in during the last twenty years of her life. I needed to know who she was before her final hours. Most urgently, I needed to finally accept who she had been. As I stood in Diane's bedroom, it became clear that she stopped living years ago. Her life had been reduced to four walls, DVDs, two laptop computers, a television, books, records, and a walker wedged into a ten-by-ten room. Her bed still smelled of urine from incontinence and her inability to make it to the bathroom three feet away. Her husband, Marcus, was ninety years old with dementia, and, while physically fit, was in no position to help. I threw out old medicine, prescriptions, expired vitamins, syringes, needles, blood pressure monitors, blood sugar strips, and broken jewelry. I cleaned her bathroom, scrubbed the sink, tub, and shower. Marcus allowed me to take a few photos, scarves, and a couple of purses. All of the designer bags, perfume, shoes, diamonds, boots, and hats Diane had once been so proud of were long gone. She had nothing.

The stress of her illness and rapid death stole my voice. For a few days, I was unable to speak above a whisper. It was like my soul was preparing my tongue to utter new words. *My mother is dead*. My kids also needed language. I told them to carry their grandmother in their heart. My mother's death was sad, but it did not change much for me. She had been gone most of my life, and now she was really gone.

2017 was such a year of loss. In September, Ann fell and fractured her hip. I began prepping August and Cherish that Grandma Ann might be going to glory sooner rather than later. I wanted to get out in front of another discussion about death. August was still processing my mother's death in February, and I didn't want him to be blindsided by her demise. Cherish wanted to know why Ann might die. I explained that her brain wasn't working that well and would eventually tell her organs to stop working. We did not know when and tried every means, including cannabis oil and edibles, to stimulate her appetite and keep her going. Nothing worked.

The day the hospice nurse called to say, "This is it," I grabbed the kids and rushed over to the boarding care where Ann resided. While we waited for the oxygen tanks to arrive, I told August and Cherish it was time to let Grandma Ann go.

"Bye, Grandma Ann." They each kissed her cheeks.

Kisha arrived quickly and took August and Cherish with her, so I could spend time alone with Ann in her last hours.

Since I had her all to myself, I climbed into bed next to her, careful not to put my weight on her fragile body. I shared what the therapist told me all those years ago when I was in law school. "You were my mother all along. Thank you."

Ann had been a constant presence for me, my children, and my friends, and I couldn't have asked for a better mother. I would miss her more than I missed Henry, more than I missed my parents. The only complaint I had was that she did not let me play baseball when I was eleven. It was petty of me to bring it up, but I didn't want to leave anything unsaid. While I rambled, Ann looked at me and nodded. High on morphine, I don't know if she understood or even cared about my foolishness.

I was grateful for our time together and gently massaged her feet, legs, and arms. Her cocoa-brown skin was smooth and soft like butter. Ann had no cellulite or wrinkles. At ninety-two years of age, she could have easily passed for seventy.

After a while, Helen and Kareem arrived. I said one last goodbye and went home. Ann Renotha Robinson Hawthorne died from late stage Alzheimer's disease on November 19, 2017, joining her husband of sixty-five years and daughter, Diane. Her best friend and sister, Ethel, would also be waiting for her. Ann's love and devotion to me and Kareem was at the heart of my decision to adopt. She supported my writing endeavors, and when I was in graduate school writing a thesis about the intersectional experience of Black women in the Black Panther Party, Ann encouraged me to tell Black women's stories. Now, I had to finally prepare myself to be my own mother.

Epilogue

I spent a long time looking for representation in parenting, and this book is in your hands because one woman seeking to be a mother was looking for answers. I thought information for mothers would be race-neutral but it wasn't. Coming up empty-handed in my search for information about Black mothers forced me to reconcile how other single, non-rich, Black women achieved motherhood.

This erasure spans socioeconomic and geographic barriers, touching every Black woman in our society. Even the baddest mama jama of them all, tennis phenomenon and twenty-three-time Grand Slam winner Serena Williams encountered unconscious racial bias after the birth of her daughter. Shortly after delivering her baby girl, Serena battled life-threatening pulmonary embolisms, a ruptured wound at the site of her C-section, and a large blood clot in her abdomen. She emerged as the definition of strength and credited her survival to her wealth and status, understanding that if she were nothing more than Serena Williams from Compton, she may have died. Her story has raised awareness that Black women in the United States die in childbirth or pregnancy-related incidents at a rate of *over three times that of white women.*

A short time later, the BBC ran an article headlined "Serena Williams: Wimbledon Finalist at 36 and a Mum—How Has She Done It?" Serena's hard work to balance career and motherhood should have been the focus of this article. Instead, readers were treated to 2013 Wimbledon champion Marion Bartoli's comment, "She is not a human, she is a hero," reminding us all that extraordinarily successful Black mothers aren't reality, they're otherworldly. Racism as veiled compliments for Black folks was nothing new. Society could not imagine us as disciplined, hard workers committed to perfecting our craft. Rather, strong Black women must be super Negroes with mythical powers who white people could safely cheer for because they were rare enough to be unthreatening. The inhumanity of this gaze is the problem and exactly the point I hoped to make with this book. Motherhood is so white and in need of a revolution. Thank you, Serena, for sharing your story and making the experience of Black motherhood visible to mainstream culture.

Women of any race shouldn't have to be superstars for our status as mothers to be respected, no matter what each woman's path to motherhood is. Choosing adoption is a constant reminder that there are myriad ways to become a mother—adoption, IVF, surrogacy, biological, or stepparent. All mothers, be they lesbian, heterosexual, Black, white, Asian, Latina, queer, transgender, nonbinary, or disabled, have struggles, and we need to support each other. We each have the same dream of building better families, and this is possible, as long as we recognize and respect each other.

I live this truth each day with the white mothers at my children's school. Over the past seven years, I have developed genuine friendships with these amazing ladies. We openly discuss universal issues of parenting and have hard conversations about race, gender, equity, and inclusion at school and in the world. We share similar values and strive to understand each other's positions when there are social or political differences. We support each other and have grown our community. These women see me not as some random single Black mother, but as a fellow member of all that is good, bad, and ugly in motherhood. These women are as much my village as my Black mom friends.

Hopefully, sharing my journey to adoption and how I learned to become a single mother on my own terms will accomplish two goals: encourage more women to choose how to curate a family and begin to bridge the racial divide that currently encapsulates motherhood. For my Black sisters who are auntie-mommies or cousin-mommies, thank you for providing crucial support for children in your family or neighborhood. And for those without children, adopting a child you do not know is not a sin and not just for rich or white people. It is a gift, and only you know if you are ready to take the plunge. This is your life, your money, and your time. Do what feels right *to you* and block out the cultural noise and expectations of how a single Black woman becomes a mother.

For my white sisters, Black mothers have a lot of child-rearing experience and plenty to say about the state of preschool, family leave, healthcare, nutrition, bullying, video games, and our socio-economically segregated school system. If we coalesced around even one of these issues, it would ease the emotional and financial burden of parenting we all experience. Also, be aware of your privilege and seek to build community with all mothers, regardless of race, religion, or socioeconomics. This is one way we can become true allies for diversity and inclusivity, while simultaneously respecting and acknowledging our unique perspectives. And should you decide to adopt transracially, love does not conquer all. You must do your homework and become culturally competent about your child's heritage.

Remember, I am not special. I essentially wrote my way out of a narrative of drug-addicted parents, abandonment, and Black adoption. I hit the reset button, and you can too. So, if the mommie-jones comes down on you, satisfy it any way you like. There are many ways to become a family. You have choices, and you will find the path that is right for you.

Stories of
Parenting So Black

Motherhood, which was the most natural experience for me despite the challenges of getting there, is often divided into two worlds, one Black, one white. How can any of us raise compassionate children in the Trump era if white women are unable to appreciate the intersectional experience of Black mothers? What is the path forward for diverse families in a world where our very existence is erased?

Out of necessity, we create spaces to showcase more realistic portraits of Black women in all of our iterations. One example of this conscious creation was comedienne and actress Kym Whitley's 2013 reality series, *Raising Whitley*, about her unplanned adoption of a baby boy and the village she assembled to help raise him. The series was hilarious and spoke to the communal nature of Black people. The OWN network carried the show and openly catered to a Black female demographic, who eagerly embraced the representation.

Black mommy blogs tell the stories of Black women at the intersection of motherhood and career. These websites offer content for Black women when we can't find it anywhere else. How refreshing it has been to discover a home for mommies who look like me. How disappointing it is in the twenty-first century to know that if I want to read about mommies who look like me, my choices are limited to the Blacks-only section or woke white feminist blogs who curate diverse material and alternate perspectives in an era where transracial adoption of Black kids is all the rage. In many cases, despite their best intentions, the stories shared by white adoptive parents of Black kids feel like an attempt to appropriate the parenting space by either whining about their privilege, fretting over what to do when love fails to conquer all, or exalting how special they are for helping the less fortunate—often with little acknowledgement of Black adoptive mothers, fathers, and other families of color.

To help correct this lack of representation, especially in the adoption community, I interviewed scores of non-celebrity single Black parents, who created families on their terms. Here are a few of those profiles. In their own words, they describe their journey to adoption.

Nikki Godfrey

I asked my cousin Nikki Godfrey to share her story for two reasons. The first is that she wasn't even thirty years old when she began the adoption process. The second is that we were adopting boys at the same time. Though my son, at six months old, was placed with me three weeks before hers was born, she and I will forever share a special bond through adoption.

Nikki is a go-getter. She holds real estate licenses in four states, worked at ESPN affiliates in three states, and works in promotions for a major university. A smart and resourceful woman, I remain in awe of Nikki for adopting a newborn before she turned thirty years old. She is such an inspiration and took on the responsibility of motherhood at time when young people are usually out clubbing and ruining their credit. At least, that's what I was doing.

When did you know you were ready to become a parent through adoption?

I think I always knew that I would be an adoptive mother. I had a babysitter who adopted four children with special needs, and I admired her and what she was doing. As a child, I tried to encourage my mother to adopt, so it came naturally to me. I knew it was time for me when I began hearing a voice in my head, seeing constant reminders of the beauty of adoption, and having that urge in my subconscious. It was too strong to ignore.

Were you single or married at the time you decided to adopt?

I was super single at the time.

Who did you tell first? Why that person?

I was hesitant to tell people at first because I knew they wouldn't understand why I wanted to adopt. I told my mom, and she was supportive, didn't really ask questions, and I think she thought it was a phase or something that I would change my mind about.

Did you know people who adopted before you did? Did this influence your decision to adopt?

I connected with a young lady who decided to adopt as a single

Black female a few months before I made my decision. She told me about her story, the realities of adoption, and how she was making it work. Her story was influential, because she let me know that it was possible and that I wasn't crazy for wanting to pursue adoption as a single Black female.

Did you research adoption before beginning the process?
I did a lot of research on adoption but found there weren't that many resources that spoke to my needs...first as a Black female and secondly as a single female. There are a *ton* of resources for married couples and white people and those wanting to pursue international adoption, but a real lack of resources when it came to materials that spoke to people who looked like me!

How did you decide between public and private adoption?
I chose a private route to adoption, though I was open to either when I made my choice to adopt. The main reason I chose that option was that I connected with a great adoption facilitator at a private agency who was awesome in speaking to me about the process, addressing my concerns, and being real about what I would face. Because of that personal connection, and a referral from a friend who had used the same facilitator, I moved forward with them.

What did you expect the adoption process to entail? Were there any gaps in your expectations?
I expected the process to entail a ton of paperwork, legal matters,

and red tape. I also expected it to last a very long time. That wasn't the case for me. Well, there was a lot of paperwork and a ton to ensure that all legalities were covered, but it wasn't as bad as I thought. I think the only thing that took me by surprise was the emotional roller coaster you go through during the entire process. It's not for the faint of heart…

Did your social worker or agency adequately educate you about the children who were available for adoption?
No. My facilitator was more birth-mother friendly. She educated birth mothers about families choosing adoption, and the birth mother would reach out to contact you to determine if you were a good fit for what they wanted for their child.

From beginning to placement, how long did you have to wait to be matched with a child?
I was matched within a month, and the baby was here three months later.

Did you have to take your child for visits with his/her birth family or siblings? Where were these visits? What was that experience like?
No, I lost contact with my son's birth mother after his first birthday. I agreed to send pictures, letters, and visit. I sent pictures and tons of updates, but didn't hear much communication. She moved around a lot, and eventually we lost touch.

Was your family supportive of your decision to adopt?

Initially, I think everyone was surprised, but after that wore off, they were certainly supportive, and once the baby was here, I think they were more excited about him than I was!

After your child was placed, did your family offer support? If so, in what capacity?

Of course! They immediately came to visit to offer assistance in caring for the baby and providing for his needs. We were overwhelmed with love and support.

What tips would you offer prospective adoptive parents in managing family fears and/or myths about adoption?

I would say that the family fears are normal and are only coming from a place of concern for you. You have to manage it, not let their fears and concerns get to you, and know that ultimately once they see you have thought things through, have a plan, and know what's to come, they will support you.

Were your friends supportive of your decision to adopt?

I would say probably not. My friends said all the right things, but their actions were different, and they withdrew. They did not know how to handle my changing lifestyle and what it would mean for them and their place in my life. That part was tough.

After your child was placed, did your friends offer support? If so, in what capacity?

I think my friends were as supportive as they could be. They remained a bit distant, but sent gifts, and I felt their love. It took a few months for them to come around.

What was the best advice you received from your social worker/agency?

That everything would unfold the way it was supposed to…and that God had a special baby waiting on me.

How did you prepare for the arrival of your child?

I purchased very few items. I got some hand-me-down clothes from my cousin. I had an interview with a pediatrician and met with an attorney to know what to expect during the finalization process.

Were you worried about adopting the mythical *crack baby*?

Yes, and actually the first baby I was matched with wasn't a crack baby, but the mother had been drinking alcohol during the pregnancy. I passed on that opportunity. I did receive the birth mother's medical records prior to the delivery of my son.

Did you have a gender preference?

I wanted a girl, but God had other plans…

Did you experience any backlash over your gender choice?

My family thought it would be easier for me to raise a girl as I was a single female, but couldn't imagine any other baby once he was here.

How has your life changed since the placement of your child?

Dramatically! Whew, kids have a way of turning everything upside down, to be honest. I learned a whole new meaning of love and also of fear. It made me face my own mortality and yet appreciate the beauty that is life. I had to become more structured and try to implement a schedule to my daily activities. I had to be more organized and more calculated in my decisions, realizing they all had an impact on the life of another person!

Was it difficult to find community for your new family?

I think I made it more difficult than what it really was because I was self-conscious. The hardest community was the church, as they wanted and highlighted the traditional family model. I purposely involved myself and my son in activities (i.e., baby gym classes, Mommy and Me groups) so we could get out and meet people.

What might never occur to a prospective adoptive parent as they're beginning the process?

Hmm…it never occurred to me that the questions would be so

hard. Now that I have a school-age child, answering the questions is the tough part. And I don't have the answers. I have not discussed adoption with my son, and prior to the process, I never thought I would have an issue talking to him about it. I don't "not" talk about it, and I answer questions as they come up, but it's hard. I specifically hate the doctor's office when I can't answer questions about family medical history.

What event or situation happened that you did not expect?
I'm never ready for the comments I get from people about adoption; they range from folks saying that my son doesn't look like me or his brothers to folks telling me how "lucky" he is to have me. I didn't expect that adoption and my decision would be such a big deal to so many people. It's a way of life for us and there's nothing unique or crazy about it.

Is there anything you want to share that I did not ask?
I'm excited this book exists, and I know it will be helpful. It's the resource I wish I had!

Carla

Carla is a former social worker who lives in Los Angeles. She is currently married and looking forward to retirement.

When did you know that you were ready to become a parent through adoption?

Around the age of twenty-nine. I wanted to be a mother, but did not want to give birth. My thought was that there are children here on earth who have been born and one of them belongs to me. I was pretty certain about this. My thoughts and desire to adopt were met with skepticism, criticism, and some lightweight shaming by family and friends.

Were you single or married at the time you decided to adopt?

I was single. I had recently ended a somewhat serious relationship, and the two of us were going back and forth about getting back together. My wanting to adopt was a deal breaker.

Who did you first tell you were going through the adoption process? Why that person?

My mother. I thought she would be supportive and excited. Wrong.

Did you know people who adopted before you did? Did this influence your decision to adopt?

I did know people who had adopted, but no one my age and only one single mother. There were relatives in my family through adoption, but from childhood, it was sort of an unspoken rule that it was not to be discussed. None of the people I knew who were either adopted or had adopted influenced my decision to adopt.

Did you research adoption before beginning the process?

Nah. I was spirit led. Other than learning about adoption through One Church One Child and PS-MAPP, I was flying by the seat of my pants.

How did you decide between public and private adoption?

I chose the public route because I thought it was safer for me and my unknown child. I thought the public route would prevent any *stolen baby* situations slapping me in the face in the later years. Also, the thought of *paying* for a baby or child turned my stomach. Plus, I couldn't have afforded that.

What did you expect the adoption process to entail? Were there any gaps in your expectations?

I expected a very long wait. The wait was not long at all—almost a year to the day I ended my PS-MAPP class, my social worker called me and said, "We think we have a match." I expected to receive a lot of information about my child from birth; I expected that his foster parents would have lots of pictures and a nice baby book and wonderful stories to share. Not so much. I wouldn't say that I experienced any gaps between my expectations and what really happened.

Did your social worker or agency adequately educate you about the children who were available for adoption?

Lord, yes. The primary social workers that I had the pleasure of working with from beginning to end were nothing short of perfection. Wanda Logan and Darcy Sanchez—social work is their calling.

From beginning to placement, how long did you have to wait to be matched with a child?

Approximately twelve months and three weeks. Spirit led. Spirit filled.

Did you have to take your child for visits with his/her birth family or siblings? Where were these visits? What was that experience like?

No, my son and I never saw any of his birth family members together; by the time I came on the scene, the court was not ordering visits. I sometimes feel bad about that. I would have loved to have met them (no fairy-tale ideas about being one big happy family), just because they are my son's people.

Did you interact with your child's foster parent? Please describe those meetings.

I met my son in his second home. I have such a deep love and respect for those parents that to this day, we remain close. The foster mother guided me, encouraged me, and loved me and my son through it all. As my son grew, we continued to visit their home, invited them to our family functions, and sent cards commemorating special occasions. I also sought out and met my son's first foster mother; I went to her home to get information (and maybe a picture) about my son as there was none in the DCFS records. I brought one of two pictures that existed of him as a child under one, and she asked me if she could have it. She took not one picture of this baby that came to her home from the hospital, that she had in her home for *nine* fucking months. That's all I have to say about that.

Was your family supportive of your decision to adopt?

Eh, there was some expressed interest. I think my parents thought I wasn't serious, even as I went through PS-MAPP and talked about adoption ad nauseam. When I brought him to my parents' home for a hot minute during one of our visits, there was mild interest. Then the week after my son and I became a family, my mother said to my face, "Why did you adopt a child? Now you have a ball and a chain." That shit still makes my stomach hurt when I think about it. I was expecting my mother to be all over my son, as she had been with my stepsister's first child. With my child, the initial silence was deafening. My parents came around eventually. It may have taken a good two years for them to treat him like I thought he should have been treated. Now, they are all over him, like brown on rice. But the initial comments and interactions, or lack thereof, have stayed with me, and it still pains me to know how my parents thought about my baby boy, obviously.

After your child was placed, did your family offer support? If so, in what capacity?

My mother offered half-assed support; she bought him a used dresser. My mother's good friend gave us our baby shower. My mother didn't seem to enjoy herself, though, as I recall. My two oldest sisters—I had to beat them fools back. One came over nearly every day with some sort of toy, and she was the one I got my "doctor mom" lessons from. The second oldest was all about taking him places—fun and games. There were several family members (my grandparents especially) who gave money like crazy. An uncle used to babysit for me in-home regularly when I worked at night. So, yes, I did have family support…a lot of it. But where I was actually expecting it to come from, it did not… in the beginning.

What tips would you offer prospective adoptive parents in managing family fears and/or myths about adoption?

Have real sit-down conversations with the people that they expect to play important roles in their child's life. Talk to them about Erik Erikson's stages of development, Abraham Maslow's hierarchy of needs. Discuss how many of our children come into the system. And above all else, talk about reasons, feelings, and behaviors. Talk to folks about children not having a choice in being adopted and talk to folks about how children should not have to be "grateful" for adults doing their jobs as parents. Remind ALL your people about all the assholes in their own families and ask how they would want those people treated, talked about, dealt with, etcetera, especially when folks want to start talking about our children's birth parents or our children themselves. Remind folks about ALL of the embarrassing family issues in their families and would they want that information spread around, and how would they feel if someone even asked. Our children are to be respected and protected. Tell them to buy books about adoption. Buy children's books about adoption (those are usually shorter) and give them to the adults to read. It may give them a better understanding of the child's perspective.

Were your friends supportive of your decision to adopt?

Yes indeed! Every single one of them. I don't have a lot, but the ones I have are pure GOLD!

After your child was placed, did your friends offer support? If so, in what capacity?

Yes. Purchasing everyday household stuff that mothers need, but don't know it until they need it. They taught me about buying certain clothes for my son (cute but no ironing needed), snacks, what to look for in toys, what to expect at bath time/meal time, etc.; taught me how to dress (cute, but comfy), what to have in the car, by the bedside, in the bathroom, etc.

What was the best advice you received from your social worker/agency?

Advocate for your child at every turn and with everyone, including schools, doctors, family members, and so on.

How did you prepare for the arrival of your child?

I found a pediatrician, a pediatric dentist, an ophthalmologist (all Black men), and a babysitter (she was sent by God). I child-proofed my second-floor apartment and started looking for a house to buy. I turned my spare room into his room and decorated it with a border that had sailboats, cars, trucks. I bought a lot of children's books, told my friends and family my life was changing and I would not be available at the spur of the moment.

Were you worried about adopting the mythical *crack baby*?

I loathe that term. I just cannot even respond.

Did you have a gender preference?

Yes, I knew I was destined to have a son since the age of fifteen. Again, I was spirit led.

Did you experience any backlash over your gender choice?

Mildly. *Why don't you want a girl? Girls are more fun. What are you going to do with a boy?*

How long did it take to finalize your adoption?

Fifteen months; not long at all.

How did you feel while you were waiting for the adoption to finalize?

For the most part, I didn't think too much about it. There were occasions when I would have low-key panic fantasies, like, What if they (the birth family, the family that was planning on adopting him before me, the social workers, white people…) try to take him from me? What if they think I am not fit because…fill in the blank (I don't make that much money, I don't urinate standing up, I don't let him watch Disney movies, I don't have a bachelor's degree, I don't accept any bullshit explanations/half-baked logic/ just-in-case scenarios/inappropriate, disrespectful language from any social worker, educator, therapist, mental or physical health, doctor, etc. who tells me to put my son on medication or refers to him as a *crack baby*…the list goes on and on 'til the break of dawn). Most of the time this wasn't a problem, because I was usually too tired to think past "gotta get up and do this all over again tomorrow."

How has your life changed since the placement of your child?

It became richer, fuller, happier, crazier, more chaotic, sometimes scary when I was the one who had to make major decisions on my own that directly affected my son. Less time for myself; eating, bathing, toileting, and entertainment for me changed completely. Even the process of caring for myself when I had a bad cold had to be modified.

Was it difficult to find community for your new family?

No, not at all. God has taken my son and me and wrapped us in love and protection. Our little family was so spirit led, it sounds like I am fantasizing when I speak of how wonderful things turned out for us, sometimes at the most challenging times.

Are you active in the adoption community?

Absolutely. I continue to teach classes at community colleges for foster parents. I also am a PS-MAPP trainer and teach those classes approximately twice a year.

What might never occur to a prospective adoptive parent as they're beginning the process?

For the parent to have an easy road. Parenting is challenging.

Adding adoption to that, a status that affects the biological, psychological, phonological, ecological, and sociological aspect of every person in the family—if one is conscious and caring—keeps you wide awake.

What event or situation happened that you did not expect?
My sister (and her husband), whom I love dearly but was not particularly close to, stepped in and stepped up like knights in shining armor. They became my son's other parents. I never dreamed this would occur, and now, I cannot imagine how our lives would have been without them in it as up close and personal as they were and still are.

Evelyn

A corporate dynamo, Evelyn Turner became a foster/adoptive mother on July 6, 1999. She was thirty-seven years old and a fixture at Xerox Corporation in El Segundo, California. Though her family lived three hundred miles away, her son couldn't have come into her life at a better time. Evelyn had just moved into a challenging assignment as a customer account  manager and was then promoted and transferred ten months later to Houston, Texas. Shortly thereafter, on December 24, 2001, she was given another honor: a special meeting in the judges' chambers in Alameda County, where she formally adopted her four-year-old son.

Two years later, Xerox downsized Evelyn's position, and she and her son relocated back to Southern California. Unemployed, Evelyn spent seven months bonding with her son, who was an active kindergartner. She describes this time as "amazing," stating, "I wanted to ensure that he had a personal touch during his school year."

Not one to sit idle, Evelyn accepted a position with Pitney Bowes in 2003, where she is currently a human resource manager. She loves her job and in May 2008, earned a master of science degree in human resources from Chapman University. She still travels extensively and relies on her strong network of family and friends to support her now teenage son.

When did you know that you were ready to become a parent through adoption?

I have always known that I wanted to adopt a child. I wanted to make a difference in a child's life.

Were you single or married at the time you decided to adopt?

I was single.

Who did you tell first? Why that person?

I actually told everyone that if I wasn't married by the time I was twenty-seven, I would adopt. Now that I reflect on that statement, at the age of twenty-seven, I was nowhere near prepared to be a

parent. So, ten years later, I made the decision that I could finan-
cially raise a child; however, I still wasn't emotionally prepared.
When I decided to go through the courses and contacted the
County agency, I knew that I was ready. I had already prepared
myself mentally to share my home and my life and be a mom.
I communicated with my close circle of friends because I knew
I would need their support. I had everything lined up before
moving to the next stage of my life as a parent.

**Did you know people who adopted before you did? Did
this influence your decision to adopt?**
I did not know of anyone who was adopted.

Did you research adoption before beginning the process?
I researched the process of going through the state as well as
going through the agency. What I found remarkable was the
primary focus of adopting through an agency was the money. I'm
not sure that placement was the primary focus versus supporting
the family unit.

How did you decide between public and private adoption?
I chose to have a private adoption through the foster care system.
I felt that many of the children available through foster care
needed a home. I knew the parental rights were terminated and
felt my son could open the door at a later age. I wanted to adopt
an African American boy because the primary focus for many

people has been girls. I felt that I could be a mom and provide my son a loving and supportive environment with a circle of male friends as a support network. He still has people that he can go to and have a male perspective in life.

What did you expect the adoption process to entail? Were there any gaps in your expectations?

I knew that I would have to go through the foster/adopt process; I completed everything through the private agency because I missed the class offered through the County. I completed the entire process prior to my son being placed with me, however, when I relocated to Houston, Texas, there was limited communication with the agency. I had to repeat all of the courses over again, this process was extremely stressful being in a different city with no family and needing to go through an eight-week course in a new city during the evenings. I had an amazing support system from my coworkers that took care of my son while I went through the process.

Did your social worker or agency adequately educate you about the children who were available for adoption?

No, unfortunately, the agency that I worked with was only concerned about the financial aspect of the adoption process. It quickly opened my eyes about the entire process. When I moved to Houston, Alameda County partnered with Harris County to complete the placement process. The social worker was very supportive and offered a lot of insight.

From beginning to placement, how long did you have to wait to be matched with a child?

I went through the foster/adopt class through a private agency. I already knew about the child that I was going to adopt. I only needed to obtain the certification, which took about three to four months. The social worker in Alameda County lobbied for me to have my son placed with me in Southern California. She had the placement handled quickly. I flew to Oakland to pick up my son the following week.

Did you have to take your child for visits with his/her birth family or siblings?

No, the parental rights were already terminated when my son was placed. The foster parents actually brought my son to my home so that I could get acquainted with him and spend some time together. It was a nice bonding process, and I realized at that time that I wanted to go through the process no matter what obstacles came into play.

Did you interact with your child's foster parents? Please describe those meetings.

Yes, the foster parents sent me photos of my son with captions. When they brought him to see me, we bonded pretty well.

Was your family supportive of your decision to adopt?

Yes, they embraced my son quickly. My family was all in.

After your child was placed, did your family offer support? If so, in what capacity?

Yes, however, I lived in a different city than my family. My friends in Southern California were a huge help in the process; they offered childcare assistance, day care, whatever I needed. Even today they are still part of the process in assisting any way they can.

What tips would you offer prospective adoptive parents in managing family fears and/or myths about adoption?

The biggest concern was the birth families finding me and concerns about ADHD, HIV, and detachment problems. I did not have a big problem with fears or myths; however, I also had some family history that was provided by my son's former case worker.

Were your friends supportive of your decision to adopt?

Yes, though some questioned why I wanted to give up my freedom.

After your child was placed, did your friends offer support? If so, in what capacity?

Everyone was very supportive of my little guy. I had people that coached me about being a parent and shared information about identifying myself as Mom so that my son could attach to me as Mom. People continue to help support me with sleepovers, carpools, gifts, and general information on being a parent. My friends sponsored a baby shower for me and purchased everything that I needed: clothes, toys, entertainment system, videos, etc.

What was the best advice you received from your social worker/agency?

Love your bundle of joy; adoption is a choice to be a parent. Have fun!

How did you prepare for the arrival of your child?

My friends were supportive in providing me with a day bed, I purchased bedding, clothes, and had the room set up for him to enjoy.

Were you worried about adopting the mythical *crack baby*?

My son's parents were substance abusers; however, I haven't seen many signs of withdrawal, etc. When he came to me, he was nineteen months and had no signs of the effects.

Did you have a gender preference?

Yes, male.

Did you experience any backlash over your gender choice?

Yes, all of my friends wanted to know why I chose a boy. Why not a girl that can bond with you later in life? I told them that girls always have an easier life. I wanted to make a difference in a boy's life; African American boys have the hardest time in America. They are always a suspect in the minds of others. I want to change the life of one person.

How long did it take to finalize your adoption?
From placement on July 6, 1999 until December 24, 2001.

How did you feel while you were waiting for the adoption to finalize?
Anxiety set in, and I reconsidered whether I wanted to complete the process. Why would I want to adopt a child as a single woman when that child could potentially go to a family with a mom and a dad?

After placement of your child, how has your life changed?
The financial burden of day care, etc. when he was smaller and now attending private school has had a huge impact financially.

Was it difficult to find community for your new family?
Our community centers on classmates that my son has engaged with since the first grade. He continues to be involved in friendships over the past ten to twelve years. I am also friends with the parents and many of them are single. We support one another with sleepovers and ride sharing.

Are you active in the adoption community?
I am currently on the board of an outreach community organization in Atlanta.

What might never occur to a prospective adoptive parent as they're beginning the process?

The cost of private school when you're living in a community with substandard educational systems. I needed to find a school that had pride in its community and supported minority students.

What event or situation happened that you did not expect?

Being required to take the foster/adoption course over when I moved to Houston, and the threat of not being able to obtain the adoption assistance benefit after relocating to a pricey neighbor while having to pay for preschool.

Reading Group Guide

1. Describe Nefertiti's relationship with her parents, Diane and Harold, and her grandparents, Ann and Henry. How do you think these relationships formed Nefertiti's first views of parenthood and what it means to be a parent?

2. How did your own upbringing influence your take on what it means to be a parent? What are some of the lessons you've learned through your childhood experiences that influenced how you do or would parent today?

3. What was Nefertiti's experience with "Black adoption," and how did it impact her choices later in life?

4. Nefertiti describes how, suddenly, the stirrings of motherhood turned into an overwhelming desire to pursue becoming a

parent. If you are a parent, what moved you to make that decision? Which path to parenthood did you choose?

5. Put yourself in Nefertiti's shoes—if you were telling your family and friends that you've decided to adopt a Black son from the foster care system, how do you think they would react? Were you surprised by the stereotypes and prejudices Nefertiti faced both from within and outside her own community? Speak on what you imagine that experience was like for her.

6. Describe the different hurdles Nefertiti had to jump to formally adopt her son, August, and later her daughter, Cherish. What are some of the challenges she faced during the foster/adoption process?

7. What were some of the stereotypes and fears Nefertiti had to confront while raising August in today's racially charged America? What about with Cherish? What were some of the biases Nefertiti personally faced as a single black mother?

8. As a single-parent household, how did Nefertiti provide male role models and positive examples of masculinity for August, and later Cherish? How did she confront the assertion that being raised without a father figure would affect August's masculinity or "make him soft?" What do those questions say

about the way Black men are perceived in America, both from within the Black community and by society at large?

9. *Motherhood So White* showcases many of the conversations and experiences parents of Black children face—from teaching their children about unconscious bias to explaining the traps embedded in our current cultural landscape. Speak about those conversations. Were there any that surprised you? Any that you, in your own experiences of parenthood, have or haven't had with your own children?

10. Throughout Nefertiti's story, she is often confronting the idea that, in America, motherhood equals white. How does she fight against that bias? How can we erase this stereotype and expand the view of motherhood to allow everyone to have a place at the table?

A Conversation with the Author

What inspired you to write *Motherhood So White*?

I was inspired to write a memoir because white mothers had so many avenues for support. Whether they were working moms or slacker moms or housewives, there were an abundance of books written with them in mind. I used to sigh and wonder, *Where were the mom narratives that featured moms who looked like me or addressed my unique experience as a Black mother?* This erasure did not sit well with me, and that's when I began telling my own story.

What is one of the biggest lessons being a mother has taught you?

Being a mother has taught me that asking for help is a strength. Most women raised during the second wave of feminism were taught to be strong, independent, and not need anybody. This "I can do it all" mentality has gotten us into a heap of trouble and not only hurts us physically but emotionally. Our mental health, especially for Black women, has suffered mightily, leading to depression and isolation. We need to lean on our support systems and demand assistance from policy-makers, husbands, partners, friends, and our children.

If you could wish for one thing for August and Cherish's futures, what would it be?

I continue to wish that their futures are fulfilling and that they have the strength to live out their dreams.

As a single mother to two young children, how did you find resources and a support system for you and your family?

Before becoming a parent, I did my due diligence. I looked into foster parent organizations, adoption support groups, and mom groups. Disappointed by the paltry resources for Black motherhood in general and Black adoption specifically, I filled in the gaps. I created a male community for my son, relying upon male friends and coaches to support August's, then Cherish's, emotional development. My friends from my pre-mom days continued to help me juggle two kids, and my family also pitched in. My support system doubled when the kids started school, but I still had to make the effort to seek out and nurture these new relationships. I hope that this book is the resource for mothers of children of color that I did not have.

If you could give one piece of advice to a new mother, what would it be?

You will be a better mother if you practice self-care. Putting your oxygen mask on first is crucial for your well-being and the well-being of your family.

What does your writing process look like?

I've been writing my whole life. Whether it's romance novels, women's fiction, or nonfiction, once I get an idea, I start the writing process with research. I go to the library or use the internet or talk to people to ensure that I understand the topic and then commit to putting in the time and work to offer a different slant on a common topic, like motherhood. My first drafts are typically a mess. I give myself permission to get all of my thoughts on the page without worrying about grammar, complete sentences, or cohesive thoughts. I set that aside for a few days or weeks and later create an outline. Then I write between four and five hours per day, during the day, while my kids are at school. Every now and then, if I'm on a deadline, I write late into the night.

Once I have taken my work as far as I can on my own, I ask my mentor or a trusted friend, who is usually but not always a fellow writer, for constructive criticism. After receiving notes, I get back to work and rewrite and rewrite and rewrite, ad nauseum, until it's done.

Did you find it difficult to write about some of your more personal experiences?

Yes! I am an introvert, so naturally, I only share my more personal experiences with close friends and family. And my day job as an adjunct history instructor lends itself to my being most comfortable observing people or events from a corner in the room. This observer perspective did not bode well for a memoir, and early versions were too academic. Since I wanted to connect with readers, I took a deep breath and stepped outside my comfort zone. I'm still a little nervous about all that I shared but found the experience cathartic.

What do you ultimately want readers to take away from your story?

I want readers to know that there is diversity within motherhood. Whether you are Black, white, Latinx, Asian, LGBTQ+, multiracial, single, married, differently abled, or an auntie/cousin mommy, we all have important, relevant information to share and can learn from one another. Let's respect and appreciate our differences, because there is nothing more universal than a mother's love for her child.

Selected Resources

The term *Black adoption* is my shorthand for nonlegal, informal adoption of relatives or close friends.

The term *Black divorce* is shorthand in the Black community for the nonlegal, mutually agreed upon separation between a married couple. The couple may or may not ever divorce.

PUBLICATIONS

Baker, Tamara A., NiCole T. Buchanan, Chivon A. Mingo, Rosalyn Roker, and Candace S. Brown. "Reconceptualizing Successful Aging Among Black Women and the Relevance of the Strong Black Woman Archetype." *The Gerontologist* 55, no. 1 (February 2015): 51-57. https://doi.org/10.1093/geront/gnu105.

Boustan, Leah Platt. "The Great Black Migration: Opportunity and Competition in Northern Labor Markets." *Focus* 32, no. 1 (2015). https://www.irp.wisc.edu/publications/focus/pdfs/foc321e.pdf.

Bynoe, Yvonne, ed. *Who's Your Mama?: The Unsung Voices of Women and Mothers*. Berkeley, CA: Soft Skull Press, 2009.

Child Welfare Information Gateway. Foster Care Statistics 2009. Washington, DC: U.S. Department of Health and Human Services, Children's Bureau, 2011: 9. Child Welfare Information Gateway. "Model Approach to Partnerships in Parenting (MAPP)." Accessed March 5, 2019. https://www.childwelfare.gov/topics/adoption /adoptive/before-adoption/preadoption/psmapp.

Columbus, Ogbujah. "African Cultural Values and Inter-communal Relations: The Case with Nigeria." *Developing Country Studies* 4, no.24 (2014). https://www.iiste.org/Journals/index.php/DCS/article /download/17135/17495.

Cosgrove-Mather, Bootie. "'Black' Names A Resume Burden?" CBS News, September 29, 2003. https://www.cbsnews.com/news/black -names-a-resume-burden.

Creation Ministries International. "Are Black People the Result of a Curse on Ham?" Accessed March 5, 2019, https://christiananswers.net/q -aig/race-blacks.html.

Crenshaw, Kimberlé. "Demarginalizing the Intersection of Race and Sex: A Black Feminist Critique of Antidiscrimination Doctrine, Feminist Theory, and Anti-Racist Politics [1989]." In *Feminist Legal Theory*, edited by Katharine T. Bartlett and Rosanne Kennedy, 57-80. New York: Routledge, 2018.

Crew, Spencer. "The Great Migration of Afro-Americans, 1915–40." *Monthly Labor Review* 110 (March 1987): 34. https://www.bls.gov /opub/mlr/1987/03/art5full.pdf.

Derilus, Patrick Jonathan. "Sometimes I Cry: The Toxic Hypermasculinity Of Black Men." *The Odyssey Online*, April 4, 2016. https://www .theodysseyonline.com/sometimes-cry-toxic-hypermasculinity-black -men.

Dill, Bonnie Thornton, Maxine Baca Zinn, and Sandra Patton in "Feminism, Race, and the Politics of Family Values." Institute for Philosophy & Public Policy, https://journals.gmu.edu/PPPQ/article /viewFile/861/636.

esthermsmth, "Stereotype Threat (Steele, Aronson)," in *Learning Theories*, September 30, 2017. https://www.learning-theories.com/stereotype -threat-steele-aronson.html.

FitzGerald, Susan. "'Crack Baby' Study Ends with Unexpected but Clear Result." *The Philadelphia Inquirer*, June 8, 2017. http://www.philly .com/philly/health/20130721__Crack_baby__study_ends_with _unexpected_but_clear_result.html.

Fottrell, Quentin. "Single Motherhood in America has Soared Since Murphy Brown's Feud with Dan Quayle." *Marketwatch*, September 30, 2018. https://www.marketwatch.com/story/single-motherhood -in-america-has-soared-since-murphy-browns-feud-with-dan-quayle -2018-01-25.

Fryer, Jr, Roland G. and Steven D. Levitt. "The Causes and Consequences of Distinctively Black Names." *The Quarterly Journal of Economics*, 119, no. 3 (August 2004). https://scholar.harvard.edu/files/fryer/files /the_causes_and_consequences_of_distinctively_black_names.pdf.

Goff, Phillip Atiba, Matthew Christian Jackson, Brooke Allison Lewis Di Leone, Carmen Marie Culotta, and Natalie Ann DiTomasso.

"The Essence of Innocence: Consequences of Dehumanizing Black Children." *Journal of Personality and Social Psychology* 106, no. 4 (2014): 526.

Jefferson, Cord. "Major 'Crack Baby' Study Concludes Poverty Worse for Kids Than Crack." *Gawker*, July 24, 2013. http://gawker.com/major-crack-baby-study-concludes-poverty-worse-for-ki-901254959.

Le Vine, Lauren. "Why We Need *Murphy Brown* in the Trump Era." *Refinery29*, January 26, 2018. https://www.refinery29.com/2018/01/188990/murphy-brown-reboot-feminism-trump.

McCrayer, Jenika. "My Feminism Is Black, Intersectional, and Womanist—And I Refuse to Be Left Out of the Movement." *Everyday Feminism*, May 6, 2015. https://everydayfeminism.com/2015/05/black-womanist-feminism.

McLanahan, Sara. "The Consequences of Single Motherhood." *The American Prospect*, Summer 1994. http://prospect.org/article/consequences-single-motherhood.

Millner, Denene. "The Attack on Black Single Mothers: Outrunning Stereotypes, Carrying the Burden." *MyBrownBaby*, July 13, 2015. http://mybrownbaby.com/2015/07/the-attack-on-black-single-mothers-outrunning-stereotypes-carrying-the-burden.

Minton, Melissa. "Serena Williams Says She Is 'Lucky to Have Survived Giving Birth.'" *Self*, February 21, 2018. https://www.self.com/story/serena-williams-says-she-is-lucky-to-have-survived-giving-birth.

Okie, Susan. "The Epidemic that Wasn't." *New York Times*, January 26, 2009. https://www.nytimes.com/2009/01/27/health/27coca.html.

Oxley, Sonia. "Serena Williams: Wimbledon Finalist at 36 and a Mum—

How Has She Done It?" *BBC News,* July 13, 2018. https://www.bbc
.com/sport/tennis/44794276.

Seals Allers, Kimberly. "Hollywood to Black Mothers: Stay Home." *New
York Times,* June 18, 2012. https://parenting.blogs.nytimes.com/2012
/06/18/hollywood-to-black-mothers-stay-home.

Simmonds, Yussuf J. "African Slave Castles." *Los Angeles Sentinel Newspaper,*
August 27, 2009. https://lasentinel.net/african-slave-castles.html.

Smithsonian Institution, Office of Elementary and Secondary Education.
"Life in the 'Promised Land': African-American Migrants in
Northern Cities, 1916–1940." *Art to Zoo,* December 1990. http://
www.smithsonianeducation.org/educators/lesson_plans/migrants
/ATZ_Migrants_Dec1990.pdf.

Walker, Rebecca. *Choosing Motherhood After a Lifetime of Ambivalence.* New
York: Riverhead Books, 2007.

Wilkerson, Isabel. *The Warmth of Other Suns: The Epic Story of America's Great
Migration.* New York: Vintage, 2011.

Williams, Heather Andrea. "How Slavery Affected African American
Families." Freedom's Story, TeacherServe©. National Humanities
Center. Accessed March 5, 2019. http://nationalhumanitiescenter
.org/tserve/freedom/1609-1865/essays/aafamilies.htm

Yale Graduate School of Arts and Sciences. "Seeing the Invisible:
Rethinking Stereotypes of Race and Gender." February 4, 2013.
https://gsas.yale.edu/news/seeing-invisible-rethinking-stereotypes
-race-and-gender.

MEDIA

Akitunde, Anthonia, founder. *Mater Mea* (website). https://www.matermea
.com.

Good Times. TV series, 1974–1979.

Bonerz, Peter, dir. *Murphy Brown.* Season 4, episode 2, "Uh-Oh: Part 3."
Aired September 16, 1991, on CBS.

Podcasts in Color. Accessed March 21, 2019. https://podcastsincolor
.com.

Raising Whitley. Kym Whitley, creator. Reality TV Series, 2013–2016.
http://www.oprah.com/app/raising-whitley.html.

Roots. Produced by David L. Wolper Productions and Warner Bros.
Television. 9 hr. 48min. American Broadcasting Company (ABC),
1977.

Slavery by Another Name. Directed by Samuel D. Pollard and produced by
TPT National Productions. 1 hr. 30min. Public Broadcasting Service
(PBS), 2012.

Acknowledgments

I never dreamt that my rants about the lack of parenting books for and about single Black adoptive mothers would become a memoir. While I had plenty to say about adoption, race, and gender, I had not considered how these issues played out within the context of motherhood. My agent, Kate McKean, did. She knew I had a story and challenged me to put it all on the page. Once I began writing, I quickly discovered her instincts were correct. Having been raised by grandparents, deciding to adopt, and choosing to do it alone all led to this moment. Thanks, Kate.

Without Kate, there would be no Anna Michels or Margaret Johnston, two thorough and thoughtful editors who forced me to dig into the recesses of my life. So many things came to the surface, and I hope my transparency encourages others to pursue parenting on their own terms. I had a third "silent" editor in the form of my literary BFF Jamey Hatley. We have been in the writing trenches since meeting in Victor LaValle's fiction class at

VONA in 2004. Jamey has been on this ride with me from the beginning and was able to drag/tease/cajole emotions out of me I had not expected to share. Jamey, we are still here!

Early iterations of my parenting essays were read and critiqued by the Write Sisters: crime novelist Pamela Samuels Young, Adrienne Byers, and Jane Howard-Martin. You guys consistently gave great notes, and I appreciate your understanding when I had to quit the group to focus on my kiddos.

I owe a huge debt of gratitude to Anthonia Akitunde, publisher of Mater Mea (matermea.com). She gave me and hundreds of other Black mothers a platform to share our parenting triumphs, failures, and mothering journeys. Anthonia recognized that Black mothers are not monolithic and continues to publish inspiring articles with beautiful pictures of Black families. Having my work featured on Mater Mea opened a lot of literary doors for me, including *MUTHA* magazine and editor-in-chief, Meg Lemke. Meg understood why I needed to take the parenting genre to task for being so exclusive and so white. Thanks, Meg; I haven't forgotten that I owe you an article. The *MUTHA* publication led to my being interviewed by hosts Biz Ellis and Theresa Thorn on the *One Bad Mother* podcast. Those ladies are hilarious and unbeknownst to me, Kate McKean was listening and so was Anna Michels. It was a total setup by the universe, and I am so happy the previous fifty agents passed on my project.

My mentor and friend Marguerite Archie-Hudson shared her wisdom with me about everything from my Black adoption to the political landscape to child-rearing. You are a generous fountain of knowledge, and the only way I can pay you back is to keep paying it forward.

My friends mean the world to me, and there is no way I can list everyone here. Do know that I appreciate your friendship and faith in me as I job hopped, moved, adopted, and wrote fiction and now nonfiction. I remain humbled by the love and support of my sister and best friend, Lori Williams, who introduced me to Rebecca M., who expertly guided me through the foster care and adoption process. A special acknowledgment to Fatimah P. who reentered my life just in time to bless me with my daughter. I would have been so lost without all of you.

Finally, this book would not be possible without my sweet son. You are the reason I began writing about adoption, and your sister is the reason I kept writing. I offer this memoir to both of you as a physical manifestation of my love and a reminder to trust yourselves.

About the Author

Author and memoirist Nefertiti Austin writes about the erasure of diverse voices in motherhood. Her work around this topic has been short-listed for literary awards and appeared in the *Huffington Post*, *MUTHA* magazine, *The Establishment*, Mater Mea, Essence.com, *Adoptive Families* magazine, PBS SoCal's *To Foster Change*, and PBS Parents. She was  the subject of an article on race and adoption in *The Atlantic* and appeared on *HuffPost Live* and *One Bad Mother*, where she shared her journey to adoption as a single Black woman. Nefertiti's expertise stems from firsthand experience and degrees in U.S. history and African American Studies. Nefertiti is a former certified PS-MAPP trainer, where she co-led classes for participants wanting to obtain a license to foster and/or adopt children from the foster care system. An alumna of Breadloaf Writers' Conference and VONA, her first two novels, *Eternity* and *Abandon*, helped usher in the Black romance genre in the mid-1990s.